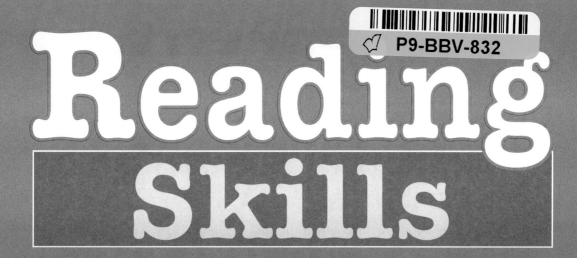

Reading Skills

Grade 2

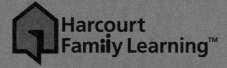

Harcourt
Family Learning™

© 2004 by Flash Kids
Adapted from *Comprehension Skills Complete Classroom Library*
by Linda Ward Beech, Tara McCarthy, and Donna Townsend
© 2001 by Harcourt Achieve
Licensed under special arrangement with Harcourt Achieve.

Illustrators: Rebecca Elliott and Janee Trasler

ISBN: 978-1-4114-0114-3

Please submit all inquiries to FlashKids@bn.com

Printed and bound in Canada

Lot #:
36 38 37 35
04/17

Flash Kids
A Division of Barnes & Noble
122 Fifth Avenue
New York, NY 10011

Dear Parent,

The ability to read well is an important part of your child's development. According to the National Institutes of Heath, students who are behind in reading in the third grade have only a 12 to 20 percent chance of ever catching up to the appropriate reading level. For this reason, it is crucial that your child master the basics of reading at an early age.

This book is designed to help your child become a better reader. The wide range of high-interest stories will hold your child's attention and help develop his or her proficiency in reading. Each of the six units focuses on a different reading comprehension skill: finding facts, detecting a sequence, learning new vocabulary through context, identifying the main idea, drawing conclusions, and making inferences. Mastering these skills will ensure that your child has the necessary tools needed for a lifetime love of reading.

Unit 1 contains activities to fine-tune your child's ability to spot facts in a story—a necessary skill for understanding a reading selection. This unit is filled with stories to test your child's understanding of how to identify facts in a story. The focus is on specific details that tell who, what, when, where, and how.

Reading for sequence means identifying the order of events in a story or the steps in a process, and understanding the relationship of one event or step to other events or steps. Unit 2 contains stories that will test your child's understanding of the order of events in a story.

Unit 3 teaches your child how to use context to learn new words. When practicing using context, your child must use all the words in a reading selection to understand the unfamiliar words. This important skill helps a reader understand words and concepts by learning how language is used to express meaning. Mastering this skill ensures that your child will become a successful independent reader.

One of the keys to learning to read well is being able to differentiate between the main point of a reading selection and the supporting details. Unit 4 will help your child learn to recognize the main idea of a story.

Drawing a conclusion is a complex reading skill because a conclusion is not stated in a reading selection. Your child must learn to put together the details from the information as if they were clues to a puzzle. The conclusion must be supported by the details in the reading selection. Unit 5 contains stories to help your child learn to draw conclusions about the passages in the book.

To make an inference, your child must consider all the facts in a reading selection. Then he or she must put together those facts and what is already known to make a reasonable inference about something that is not stated in the selection. Making an inference requires the reader to go beyond the information in the text. Unit 6 will help your child learn how to make inferences.

To help your child get the most from this workbook, encourage your child to read each reading selection slowly and carefully. Explain the purpose of each unit to your child so that he or she has a better understanding of how it will help his or her reading skills. There's an answer key at the end of this workbook. Your child can check the answer key to see which questions he or she got right and wrong. Go back to the questions your child answered incorrectly and go over them again to see why he or she picked the incorrect answer. Completing the activities in this workbook will get your child on the right track to becoming an excellent reader. Continue your child's educational development at home with these fun activities:

- Enlist your child's help when writing grocery lists.
- When preparing a meal, have your child read the recipe aloud.
- Provide entertaining reading selections for your child. Have a discussion about what he or she has read.
- Instead of reading a bedtime story to your child, have your child read a bedtime story to you!
- Write down the directions to a project, such as a gardening project or an arts and crafts project, for your child to read.
- Give your child a fun reading passage and ask him or her to draw a picture about it.
- Ask your child to read road signs and billboards that you encounter during car trips.
- Leave cute notes on the refrigerator or your child's pillow.
- Have your child write and mail a letter to a loved one.
- Ask your child to read the directions for a board game, and then play the game together.
- Bring your child to the library or bookstore so that he or she can choose which great book to read next.

Table of Contents

unit 4
Main Idea

unit 5
Conclusion

unit 6
Inference

What Are Facts?

Facts are things you know are true. Everything you read has facts in it. Read this:

> Bob was smiling. At last it was spring.

Bob was smiling. That is a fact. The time of year was spring. That is also a fact. There is one more fact you know. You know the person's name.

Try It!

Read this story. It has facts about what people used to think a long time ago.

The Earth and the Sun

Long ago a man was thinking about the sky. He had been watching the Sun for days. He began to see it in a new way. "Earth is going around the Sun," he said. At that time most people thought the Sun went around Earth. They thought Earth was the biggest and best thing in the sky.

The man said, "I must write a book. It might make people angry. But I must tell the truth." The man did write a book, but he never saw it printed. He died in 1543. The book was printed later that year.

People were angry when they read the book. They wanted to think that everything went around Earth. Today people know that the man was right.

How to Find Facts

Try to find the facts in the story. Write the facts on the lines below.

Fact 1: The man had been watching the _____ for days. (Moon, Earth, Sun)

Fact 2: The man died in the year _____. (1543, 1453, 1457)

Fact 3: The man said, "I must write a _____." (letter, story, book)

• To find facts you must know what to look for. For Fact 1 you must look for a thing the man watched. For Fact 2 you must look for a date. For Fact 3 you must look for what the man said. Read the story again. Draw a line under the words *Sun* and *book*, and under the number *1543*. They are the right answers for Facts 1, 3, and 2.

• To find the facts, read the story very carefully. If you cannot remember the facts, read the story again.

Read each story. After each story you will answer questions about the facts in the story. Remember, a fact is something that you know is true.

Seashells

Seashells come in many different shapes, sizes, and colors. Some shells grow as big as 4 feet long. Some shells are smaller than 1/2 inch long. Some shells have two sides that open like wings. Other shells are shaped like a curling tube. Shells come in all colors: white, black, brown, yellow, green, red, orange, and pink. They are like a rainbow in the ocean.

Many seashells are named for other things we know. The spider shell is one example. The spider shell has long points that look like spider legs. The comb shell has points, too. Its points are straight and close together, just like those in a comb.

_____ 1. Some shells grow
  A. rainbows
  B. 4 feet long
  C. butterfly wings

_____ 2. The smallest shells are
  A. 1/2 foot long
  B. 2 inches wide
  C. smaller than 1/2 inch long

_____ 3. Some shells are named for
  A. people who found them
  B. other things we know
  C. where they are found

_____ 4. Some seashells have
  A. arms
  B. points
  C. homes

There are two kinds of bear shells. One is called the little bear. It is a small shell. The bear-paw shell is different. It is a big shell with two parts. Each half looks like an animal foot.

Some names of shells do not make any sense. The apple shell doesn't look like an apple at all. And the dog shell doesn't look like a dog. The butterfly shell is very plain. Many other shells look more like a butterfly than that one does! But the heart shell does have the shape of a heart. Not all heart shells are red. Some are yellow. Others have brown spots.

_____ **5.** There are
  A. two kinds of bear shells
  B. three types of butterflies
  C. two kinds of apple shells

_____ **6.** The bear-paw shell has
  A. one part
  B. two parts
  C. three parts

_____ **7.** The dog shell
  A. looks like an animal foot
  B. doesn't look like a dog
  C. is yellow or red

_____ **8.** Sometimes the heart shell has
  A. brown spots
  B. a butterfly shape
  C. three points

Good Foods, Poor Names

Some foods have names that make good sense. Take an orange, for example. Its color is orange. So it seems only right to call the fruit by that name.

But what about the peanut? True, it is a kind of pea. Like other peas, a peanut grows in a shell, or pod. But a peanut is not a nut. It might seem like a nut. After all, it is small, round, and hard. But a peanut is not part of the nut family. So the name *peanut* is really not the best name for the food! Can you think of a better name for the peanut?

1. An orange gets its name because
    A. it is a round fruit
    B. it is juicy inside
    C. its color is orange

2. A peanut is a kind of
    A. pea
    B. nut
    C. pea and nut

3. A peanut grows in a
    A. shell
    B. pit
    C. skin

4. A peanut is
    A. long and soft
    B. small and round
    C. flat and square

Did you ever eat a pineapple? You might have liked its taste. But how good is its name? A pineapple is neither a pine nor an apple. It looks like a large pinecone. But it is not in the pine family. It is not in the apple family, either. What may be a better name for a pineapple?

You may enjoy grapefruit. But its name is not the best. Yes, it is a fruit. But it is not in the grape family. Grapes grow on vines. Grapefruit grow on trees. What does all this prove? The names of foods can be food for thought!

 5. A pineapple is
   A. both a pine and an apple
   B. not a pine or an apple
   C. a pine but not an apple

 6. A pineapple looks like
   A. a big pine cone
   B. a big apple
   C. a big grape

 7. A grapefruit is
   A. a grape but not a fruit
   B. both a grape and a fruit
   C. a fruit but not a grape

 8. Grapefruit grow on
   A. vines
   B. trees
   C. pines

Our Amazing Skin

Our skin is like a bag that we live in. Inside the bag our bodies are mostly water. Our water is like the water in the sea. It is very salty. Also, like the ocean, we can lose our water. The wind and the sun could take it away. Our bag of skin keeps our body's ocean from drying up.

Our skin keeps out sunshine. Too much sun can hurt us. Skin also keeps out dirt. That's important because some kinds of dirt can make us sick. Our skin feels things. It feels warm things, cold things, things it touches, and things that hurt it. A campfire feels warm. A snowball thrown in our face feels cold and hurts. A hug is the touch of another person's skin on our own.

_____**1.** Our bodies are mostly
    A. salt
    B. water
    C. skin

_____**2.** Our skin keeps our body's water from
    A. drying up
    B. getting cold
    C. smelling bad

_____**3.** Skin keeps out
    A. dirt
    B. food
    C. water

_____**4.** Our skin helps us
    A. read
    B. feel
    C. dream

Our hair is a special kind of covering. It helps keep things out of our eyes, ears, and nose. Hair is also good for keeping us warm. When we get goose bumps, our body hairs stand up. Then the hairs hold air close to our skin like a thin blanket. Hair keeps animals warm, too. Some animals have more hair than others, so they have a better blanket for cold weather.

Our nails are like very hard skin. They help keep our fingers and toes from getting hurt. Our nails aren't as strong or sharp as the nails that animals have. But they are good for scratching backs and picking up coins.

_____ **5.** Hair helps keep things out of our
    A. fingers and toes
    B. mouth and ears
    C. eyes, ears, and nose

_____ **6.** Hair is good for
    A. keeping us clean
    B. helping us stay warm
    C. keeping us from getting hurt

_____ **7.** Nails are like
    A. flat hair
    B. hard skin
    C. thin blankets

_____ **8.** Nails help keep our
    A. toes sharp
    B. fingers from getting loose
    C. toes from getting hurt

Crazy Town, U.S.A.

Towns get their names in many ways. One town in Wyoming is called Ten Sleep. People there had their own way of telling how far away a place was. They would tell how many nights one had to sleep on a trip there. This town was ten nights from three other places.

Ong's Hat, New Jersey, got its name in a funny way. A man named Jacob Ong lived in this village. He liked three things: dancing, women, and his fancy hat. One night he was at a big dance. One woman thought that he should dance with her more. Finally she grabbed his fancy hat and threw it on the floor. Then she danced all over his hat.

_____ **1.** One town in Wyoming is called
    A. Three Sheep
    B. Ong's Hat
    C. Ten Sleep

_____ **2.** Ten Sleep got its name from the
    A. name of a man who lived there
    B. way people told how far to travel
    C. river that ran through the town

_____ **3.** Jacob Ong had a village named after his
    A. dance
    B. hat
    C. mother

_____ **4.** Ong got into trouble when he was
    A. at a big dance
    B. telling a funny story
    C. talking to a man

In New Mexico there is a place called Pie Town. A man started making little fruit pies to sell at his gas station. Then the people who owned the food store got the same idea. They started selling big pies. One day a cowboy passed through town. He said, "This sure is a pie town." Pie Town became the new name.

Midnight, Mississippi, got its name from a card game. The farmers would get together to play cards. Late one night a player lost all his money. Then he bet his land, but he lost that, too. The winner looked at his watch. "It's midnight," he said. "That's what I'll call my new land!"

_____ **5.** A man sold fruit pies at his
    A. friend's house
    B. pie shop
    C. gas station

_____ **6.** Pie Town was named by
    A. a cowboy who passed through
    B. the owner of the gas station
    C. the state of New Mexico

_____ **7.** In Mississippi the farmers would
    A. make pies and sell them
    B. work for many days and nights
    C. get together to play cards

_____ **8.** The winner of the card game
    A. named his land Pie Town
    B. won at midnight
    C. lived in Alaska

An Amazing Life

Helen Keller became ill while she was still a baby. The illness caused her to lose her sight and hearing. Because she could not see or hear, she did not know how to speak. Helen was shut off from the rest of the world.

At age seven Helen was given a private teacher. Her name was Anne Sullivan. Anne was nearly blind as a child. She knew how it felt not to see. Anne taught Helen through touch. She spelled out letters on Helen's hand. The letters spelled the names of things. Anne placed those things in Helen's hand. Soon Helen knew how to spell words.

_____ 1. Helen's illness caused her to
   A. lose her taste
   B. lose her touch
   C. lose her sight and hearing

_____ 2. As a child, Helen
   A. could only whisper
   B. spoke normally
   C. was not able to speak

_____ 3. Anne Sullivan taught Helen
   A. by phone
   B. through music
   C. through touch

_____ 4. Anne spelled letters on Helen's
   A. throat
   B. hand
   C. eyes

Helen wanted to learn more. At age 10 she began to learn to speak. Her teacher spoke to her. Helen placed a finger on the speaker's lips and throat. By age 16 Helen could speak pretty well. She went to college and made top grades.

After college Helen worked to help other people who were blind. She taught them to have hope and to be brave. She wrote many books about her life. She gave speeches all over the world. She raised lots of money for those who were blind. Helen Keller became a hero to people everywhere.

_____ **5.** At age 10 Helen started to learn
    A. to speak
    B. to sing
    C. to write

_____ **6.** Helen felt a speaker's
    A. nose and ears
    B. eyes and hands
    C. throat and lips

_____ **7.** Helen wrote books about
    A. famous people
    B. her own life
    C. how the brain works

_____ **8.** Helen helped people
who were blind by
    A. raising money for them
    B. letting Anne teach them
    C. becoming a doctor

Bicycles

People who rode the first bicycles worked hard. They had to push their feet against the ground to make their bikes move. These bikes, called hobby horses, had four wheels.

Later, people began to make bikes with two wheels. The bikes were not like those seen on the streets today. People sat above the front wheel of the bikes. As they rode, their feet turned the wheel. Bicycle makers tried making big front wheels and small front wheels. They learned that bikes with larger front wheels could move faster. So they started making bikes with large front wheels and small back wheels.

_____ **1.** Hobby horses had
   A. big wheels
   B. two wheels
   C. four wheels

_____ **2.** On later bikes people
   A. sat above the front wheel
   B. pushed their feet against the ground
   C. rode a long way without stopping

_____ **3.** Bicycle makers tried making
   A. no wheels at all
   B. small front wheels
   C. rubber wheels

_____ **4.** Bikes with larger front wheels were
   A. slower
   B. faster
   C. safer

Soon the streets were filled with bikes with huge front wheels. Some bikes had wheels that were 5 feet tall. Many people were hurt when they fell off these bikes.

Later, people in England made a bike with smaller wheels. The two wheels on the new bike were almost the same size. People sat between the wheels, and their feet pushed two pedals. The two pedals moved a chain that turned the back wheel. The new bike was called a safety bike. People could ride on it without falling 5 feet to the ground. This safe bike became the model for today's bikes.

_____ **5.** The streets were filled with bikes with
  A. huge front wheels
  B. five pedals
  C. small seats

_____ **6.** In England people made a bike with
  A. two wheels of the same size
  B. three wheels on the back
  C. no handles

_____ **7.** The new bike's back wheel turned with a
  A. chain
  B. brake
  C. pedal

_____ **8.** The safety bike became a model for
  A. model trains
  B. new cars
  C. today's bikes

Working Worms

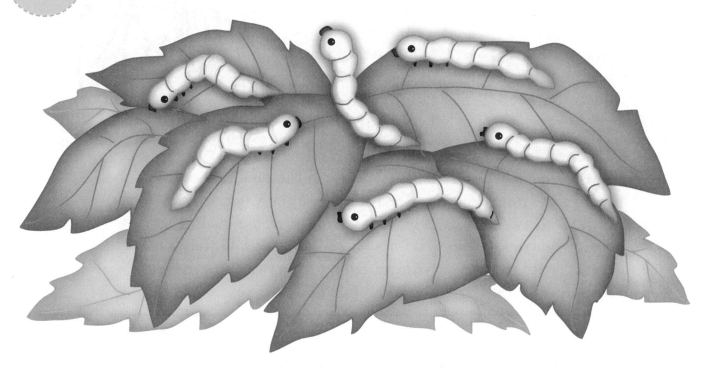

Many people think that silk is the finest cloth of all. Just touching silk can be a surprise because it is so soft. Even more surprising is the fact that silk is made by special worms.

If you visited a silk farm, you would see two things: worms and trees. Silkworms eat only the leaves of mulberry trees. So rows and rows of these trees grow on silk farms. On some farms the leaves are picked by hand. Workers gather leaves from whole branches at once. In other places machines do this work. The farmers chop the leaves. Then they feed them to their worms.

_____ **1.** Silk is a type of very fine
   A. worm
   B. tree
   C. cloth

_____ **2.** At a silk farm, there are worms and
   A. spiders
   B. cows
   C. trees

_____ **3.** Silkworms eat only
   A. silk cloth
   B. mulberry leaves
   C. apple trees

_____ **4.** On some farms the leaves are
   A. picked by hand
   B. cooked in pots
   C. left on trees

Silkworms do nothing but sleep and eat. They grow very quickly. As the worms grow, they shed their skin four times. The old skin splits and falls off.

After so much work, the worms are ready to change into moths. Each worm spins a single long thread around and around itself. This new home is called a cocoon. The thread of each cocoon is as thin as a spiderweb. The farmers steam and dry the cocoons. Then the dry cocoons go to a silk-making plant. There the threads are spun into silk yarn. The yarn will be made into soft cloth that feels like a cloud.

_____ **5.** A silkworm grows
    A. slowly
    B. smaller
    C. quickly

_____ **6.** A silkworm's skin splits and
    A. gets smaller
    B. comes off
    C. becomes wet

_____ **7.** The thread of each cocoon is
    A. thin
    B. fat
    C. red

_____ **8.** Silk cloth is very
    A. rough
    B. tight
    C. soft

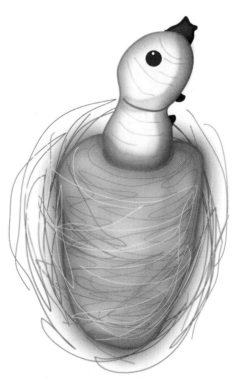

Tears and More Tears

Sometimes people cry when they are sad. Other times people cry tears of joy. But your eyes make tears all the time, whether you are crying or not. Did you know that tears help keep your eyes healthy? They keep your eyes from drying out. A special area of the eye drips all the time. It keeps the eye damp.

If you look in a mirror, you can see tiny holes in the corners of your eyes. Each hole leads to a small tube that runs to your nose. Tears run slowly into this tube drip by drip. Day and night the holes drain the tears away. If they didn't, you would always look as if you were crying!

_____ **1.** Your eyes make tears
  A. all the time
  B. only at night
  C. only when you are sad

_____ **2.** Tears keep your eyes from
  A. blinking
  B. drying out
  C. opening

_____ **3.** In the corners of your eyes, there are
  A. short brushes
  B. small hairs
  C. tiny holes

_____ **4.** Each hole leads to
  A. another hole
  B. your ear
  C. a tube

If you begin to cry, there are many more tears. The holes can't drain all of them. The extra tears spill out onto your face.

Tears help keep your eyes safe. If there is something harmful in the air, the eyes fill with tears. These tears coat your eyes. They keep the harmful air out.

Contact lenses can make the eyes too dry. Some people have to add tears to their eyes. They buy bottles of eye drops to keep their eyes damp.

_____ **5.** When you cry, there are many more
    A. tears
    B. holes
    C. drains

_____ **6.** If there are harmful things in the air,
    A. the eyes will fill with tears
    B. you will never know it
    C. most people close their eyes

_____ **7.** Tears will
    A. coat your eyes
    B. put you to sleep
    C. open your eyes

_____ **8.** Contact lenses can make the eyes too
    A. weak
    B. old
    C. dry

Writing Roundup

Read the story below. Think about the facts. Then answer the questions in complete sentences.

Today we know many facts about the Moon. Humans have traveled to the Moon and back. They have brought back soil to study.

The Moon's soil is made of rock and glass. Some of the rock is small and ground up. Other rock is in large chunks. The glass on the Moon is very tiny. Each bit is about as small as the period at the end of this sentence. In the future more trips to the Moon will be made. Then we will learn even more facts about its soil.

1. How do we know facts about the Moon today?

_____

_____

2. What is the Moon's soil made of?

_____

_____

3. How small is the glass on the Moon?

_____

_____

Prewriting

Think of an idea you might write about, such as a place you visited or an item you found. Write the idea in the center of the idea web below. Then fill out the rest of the web with facts.

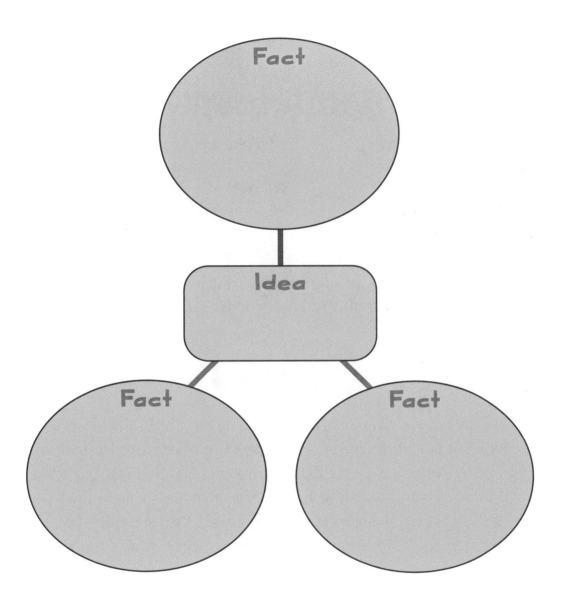

On Your Own

Now use another sheet of paper to write a story about your idea. Use the facts from your idea web.

What Is Sequence?

Sequence means *time order*. When things happen in a story, they happen in a sequence. Something happens first. Then other things happen. Then something happens last. How can you find the sequence in a story? Just look for clue words, like these:

today	Monday	then
first	after	June

Try It!

Here is a story about apples. See whether you can follow the sequence. Circle all the clue words.

Apples

People have liked apples for many years. But the New World has not always had apple trees. People carried the trees to America about 400 years ago. At first people planted trees only in the East. Later, travelers carried them west. Now apples grow in most states. We use them in pies and jellies. But most of all, we just like to eat them raw.

How to Find Sequence

Try to follow the sequence in the story about apples. On this page there are two sentences about the story. Write the number **1** on the line by the sentence that tells what happened first. Write the number **2** by the sentence that tells what happened next.

_____ Travelers carried apple trees west.

_____ People planted apple trees in the East.

• Read all the words in the two sentences above. Now read the story about apples again. Try to find the words in the two sentences that are in the story. Did you find the words *travelers* and *East* in the story? Draw a line under these two words.

• After you find the words *travelers* and *East*, find the clue words that are close by. The clue words that go with *East* are *at first*. The clue word that goes with *travelers* is *later*. The clue words tell you how to put things in a sequence. *At first* tells you that something happened at the very beginning. *Later* tells you that something happened after something else.

• If you still cannot find the sequence, try this. Look at the sentences in the story. One sentence is first. Another sentence is second, and another one is third. The sentences are in order. The action in the first sentence happened first, and the action in the second sentence happened second.

Read each story. After each story you will answer questions about the sequence of events in the story. Remember, sequence is the order of things.

King of the Worms

Jody Gerard was 10 years old when he decided he needed a job. He thought it might be fun to raise worms. He could sell them to farmers and people who fished. So in the spring, he bought many worms. Jody put the worms in clean dirt. He gave them water, leaves, and corn all summer. The worms got fat, and Jody sold many of them. But that winter he did not put them in a warm place. The cold weather killed all the worms.

The next spring Jody tried again. He bought more worms. He took good care of them. Many people bought Jody's worms. When winter came Jody took the worms inside so they would stay warm.

One day when Jody was 12, he got a letter. It was from the state of New York, where he lived. The letter said, "Everyone who sells things has to pay taxes!" Jody made only 50¢ per day selling worms. But he still had to pay part of that money to the state. Jody told many people in his town what had happened. Soon some people from a television station came to Jody's house. He told them about his problem. They showed a film on television of their talk with Jody. Many people saw it. The people began to write letters to the state. The letters said that the law was unfair. Finally the law was changed. Children like Jody can now sell things without paying money to the state.

1. Put these events in the order that they happened. What happened first? Write the number **1** on the line by that sentence. Then write the number **2** by the sentence that tells what happened next.

_____ Jody had to pay money to the state.

_____ Television people came to Jody's house.

_____ **2.** When did Jody first sell worms?
  A. when he was 10
  B. when he was 14
  C. when he was 12

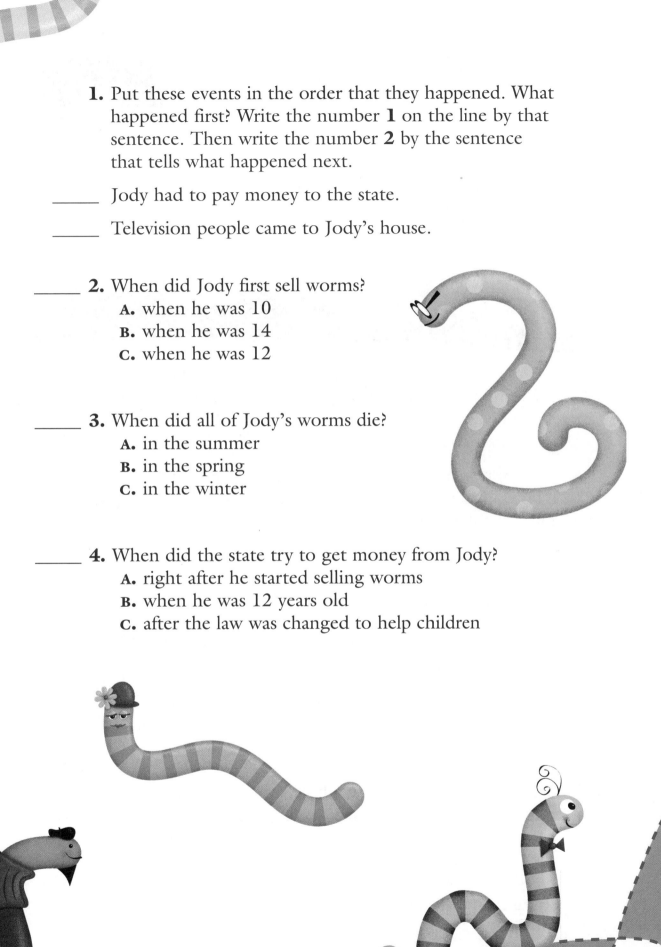

_____ **3.** When did all of Jody's worms die?
  A. in the summer
  B. in the spring
  C. in the winter

_____ **4.** When did the state try to get money from Jody?
  A. right after he started selling worms
  B. when he was 12 years old
  C. after the law was changed to help children

Making a Rose Necklace

Here is how you can make a necklace that smells like roses. First find roses that smell very sweet. Pick about four cups of rose flowers. Pick only the colored flowers. Be sure to keep the green parts out.

Then tear the flowers into very tiny pieces. Put the pieces into a bowl, and add ½ cup of cold water. Use a wooden spoon to mash the flower bits. Mash them into a smooth paste.

Next cook the rose paste in a big pot. You can use a pot made of glass or iron. Cook the paste on low heat. Watch it all the time. If the paste gets too hot and begins to boil, it will not smell good anymore. Stir the rose paste so it will not burn. The paste is ready when it sticks to the sides of the pot. Turn off the heat and let the paste cool.

When the paste has cooled, it's time to make rose beads. Squeeze the paste in your hands. It should be stiff and a little sticky. If it's still really wet, pat it with a soft paper towel. Now make little balls about 1 inch across. Then stick a big needle through each ball to make a hole. After you make the holes, put the beads on clean paper to dry. Drying them will take two or three days. Turn the beads over carefully each day. This helps them dry evenly. When the beads are dry, they are hard and black. Rub them well with a soft cloth to make them shine. Now string the beads on fishing line. The dark beads will smell of roses.

1. Put these events in the order that they happened. What happened first? Write the number **1** on the line by that sentence. Then write the number **2** by the sentence that tells what happened next.

_____ Rub the rose beads with a soft cloth.

_____ String the beads on fishing line.

_____ **2.** When do you add water to the rose flowers?
    A. before you pick them
    B. after you tear them into little pieces
    C. after the rose paste is cooked

_____ **3.** When do you cook the rose paste?
    A. before making rose beads
    B. after it is stiff
    C. while tearing the flowers into pieces

_____ **4.** When do you let the beads dry?
    A. after you put them on a string to wear
    B. after you put the needle through them
    C. before you make the little, round balls

Stunt Car Driving

A thief runs from the bank. He jumps into a waiting car and roars off. People run after him, but it's too late. He's gotten away. Or has he? Look! Another car is coming toward the thief. The car is not stopping. Crash!!! Suddenly the two cars are in flames. There's been a terrible accident.

Scenes like this in movies thrill people all the time. The accident looks real, but no one is really hurt. These scenes are done by actors called stunt people. They take the place of the regular actors in the dangerous parts.

A director hires stunt people to appear in a film. First the stunt people plan what will happen. This is called rigging the gag. They go over each part of the scene many times. The timing is very important. It may take many days to plan a stunt. The stunt people then check all the equipment. Everything must be in perfect working order.

Then it's time to begin. For a crash scene, the stunt people get into the cars. The cameras roll. At the moment of the crash, the two drivers jump from the cars. The stunt drivers are quick, and their escape does not show on the film.

The shells of two other cars are then towed to the scene. These shells look just like the cars that crashed. Dummy drivers are put into the cars. When the cars hit a trigger in the road, they burst into flames. These shells have no engines and they burn without exploding. The camera takes pictures of it all.

1. Put these events in the order that they happened. What happened first? Write the number **1** on the line by that sentence. Then write the number **2** by the sentence that tells what happened next.

_____ The thief jumped into a car.

_____ The thief ran from the bank.

_____ **2.** When do the stunt people rig the gag?
- **A.** before they do the stunt
- **B.** as they get in the cars
- **C.** at the moment of the crash

_____ **3.** When do stunt people check the equipment?
- **A.** after the shells arrive
- **B.** when they do the stunt
- **C.** after they plan the stunt

_____ **4.** When do the stunt people jump out of the cars?
- **A.** before they check the equipment
- **B.** during the crash
- **C.** after the shells are towed into place

Growing Tiny Popcorn

When Shelly Hoff was eight, a woman gave her three ears of popcorn. They were the smallest ears that Shelly had ever seen. They were about 3 inches long. That's about half as big as an ear of common corn.

Shelly wanted to grow popcorn. She took some of the seeds from the corn ears. When spring came she dug her garden. Then she put the corn seeds in water for one night. The next day she planted her corn. She put the seeds about 1 inch under the dirt.

Shelly watered her garden all summer, but she had made one mistake. She had planted the small popcorn too close to some common corn. Her new plants just grew big ears of corn.

The next year Shelly tried again. This time she made sure there wasn't any common corn nearby. The seeds came up, and the corn looked good. It didn't grow very fast. Her friends told her that corn is a hungry plant. It takes a lot of food out of the ground. So she put special food on the plants. That fall she picked a few ears of popcorn.

When spring came again, Shelly planted lots of popcorn. The corn had sun, food, and water all summer. By fall she had many small ears of corn.

Now Shelly sells her corn to flower shops. Farmers' markets and gift shops also buy it. She uses her corn money for clothes. She also saves money so she can go to college.

1. Put these events in the order that they happened. What happened first? Write the number **1** on the line by that sentence. Then write the number **2** by the sentence that tells what happened next.

_____ Shelly's plants grew big ears of corn.

_____ Shelly planted corn seeds.

_____ **2.** When did a woman give popcorn to Shelly?
  A. when Shelly was eight
  B. when Shelly was three
  C. when Shelly was seven

_____ **3.** When did Shelly put the seeds in water?
  A. before she put the seeds in the ground
  B. after she planted the seeds in the garden
  C. right before she sold the popcorn

_____ **4.** What mistake did Shelly make the first year?
  A. planting too much popcorn
  B. not giving the popcorn enough food
  C. planting the popcorn too close to common corn

A Secret King

A king wanted to see what his people were really like. So he put on rags and went for a walk. After a while he got tired and hungry. When he asked people for food, they laughed and threw rocks at him. They did not know who the poor man was.

Then the king came to an old house. A poor old man and woman lived there. They asked the king to eat with them. They didn't know he was the king. They just wanted to help a tired, hungry man. The woman made a fire. Then she brought cool water for the king to drink. While she was doing this, the old man went outside. He picked some food from the tiny garden. Then he tried to catch a chicken for supper. But the chicken ran fast, and the old man was tired. So he chose some eggs instead.

The woman cooked supper for them. When the food was ready, she put it on the table. The king was given the best food. Suddenly there was a knock at the door. The old woman opened it and saw some neighbors.

"Great king, forgive us," they said. "We threw rocks because we did not recognize you." The king was angry. "I was tired and hungry. You gave me only rocks and bad words. Get out of here!" he shouted.

The poor man and woman were afraid. The king was used to nice food, but they had given him only bread and eggs. The king said, "You gave me the best you had. Because you were kind, I will give money and food to you for the rest of your lives."

1. Put these events in the order that they happened. What happened first? Write the number **1** on the line by that sentence. Then write the number **2** by the sentence that tells what happened next.

_____ The man and woman asked the king to dinner.

_____ The king put on rags and went for a walk.

_____ **2.** When did the people of the town throw rocks?
  A. after the king stopped at the old house
  B. when the king asked them for food
  C. when the king shouted, "Get out of here!"

_____ **3.** When did the old man get the food for supper?
  A. while the old woman made the fire
  B. before the people threw rocks
  C. after the neighbors knocked at the door

_____ **4.** When did the woman give water to the king?
  A. before he dressed in rags and went walking
  B. after the neighbors came by the house
  C. after she made a fire to cook supper

You know who Snow White is. You've heard of Hansel and Gretel. But have you heard of the Brothers Grimm? If not for them, you might never have heard these tales.

Jakob and Wilhelm Grimm were the oldest of six children. Jakob was born in 1785. Wilhelm was born the next year. They were the best of friends. The brothers lived and worked together for most of their lives.

In 1798, the Grimms moved to the town of Kassel. There they finished school. Then they found jobs in the king's library. Both men loved old stories. In their free time, they searched for old folktales and songs.

From 1807 to 1814, Jakob and Wilhelm collected tales from everyone they knew. Marie Muller was a nanny. She told them the tales of Snow White, Little Red Riding Hood, and Sleeping Beauty. One day the Grimms met Frau Viehmann. She came to their house many times. She drank coffee and ate rolls. She told the Grimms more than 20 tales. Cinderella was one of them.

In 1812, the Grimms' first book of fairy tales was published. The Grimms had meant the stories for grown-ups. They were surprised when children loved them, too. The brothers wanted to find more tales. This time it was much easier. Now people would bring stories to them. The next book of tales was published in 1814. The last book of Grimm's fairy tales was published in 1857.

1. Put these events in the order that they happened. What happened first? Write the number **1** on the line by that sentence. Then write the number **2** by the sentence that tells what happened next.

_____ The brothers finished school.

_____ The brothers collected tales.

_____ **2.** When was Wilhelm Grimm born?
   A. the year before Jakob was born
   B. in 1785
   C. the year after Jakob was born

_____ **3.** When did the brothers collect tales from friends?
   A. from 1807 to 1814
   B. in 1798
   C. when they were children

_____ **4.** When was the Grimms' first book of fairy tales published?
   A. when the brothers were in school
   B. after they began working in the library
   C. from 1807 to 1814

Elephants

Elephants are the largest mammals on land. Long ago there were elephants in most countries. Now elephants live only in Africa and Asia. They are smart animals that live together and help each other.

Female elephants live in close family groups. The group is made of mothers and their babies. The young males stay with this group until they are about 14 years old. Then they leave to join a group of male elephants. The males travel in groups, but they are not as close as the family groups. Males often move from one herd to another.

A herd wakes up at 4:00 in the morning. The elephants want to start grazing before it gets too hot. They walk to a water hole and drink. The herd walks and eats about 16 hours per day. They eat grass, leaves, bark, and fruit. Sometimes they stop and take naps. At midnight the herd stops for the night. All the elephants lie down and sleep. Some of them snore.

Babies can be born at any time of the year. A baby weighs 250 pounds when it is born. It stands up 15 minutes after it's born. The herd moves slowly for the first few days. The young one walks between its mother and another female. If it gets tired, they hold it up with their trunks. By the third day, the baby can keep up with the herd. At first the little one doesn't know how to use its trunk. Sometimes it steps on it. Sometimes it even sucks its trunk like a human baby sucks its thumb.

1. Put these events in the order that they happened. What happened first? Write the number **1** on the line by that sentence. Then write the number **2** by the sentence that tells what happened next.

_____ Elephants live only in Africa and Asia.

_____ Elephants lived in most countries.

_____ **2.** When do young males join a male herd?
    A. when they are about 14
    B. in the early morning
    C. when their mothers tell them to

_____ **3.** When does a herd wake up?
    A. after it gets hot
    B. at midnight
    C. about 4:00 in the morning

_____ **4.** When are baby elephants born?
    A. in the spring
    B. during any season
    C. usually in the summer

Paper

Paper has been around for a long time. It was invented by the Chinese about A.D. 105. In the 1400s the printing press was invented in Europe. For the first time, large numbers of books could be made. Many paper mills were built.

Now we use paper for lots of things. Most of the paper goods we take for granted haven't been in use for very long. There were no paper towels or tissues 100 years ago. Paper bags were rarely used. Children in school wrote on slates, not on paper.

Each person in a rich country uses about 350 pounds of paper a year! A person in a poor country uses about 40 pounds a year. This adds up to a lot of paper and a lot of trees! It takes more than 2 tons of wood to make 1 ton of paper. The more paper we use, the more trees have to be cut down. Luckily, many kinds of paper can be reused. Egg cartons and newspapers are now made from recycled paper.

Let's take a look at how paper is made. First, of course, the trees are cut down. The logs are carried by truck to a pulp mill. Pulp mills are often built near rivers. It takes a lot of water to make paper. The bark is cut off the logs. Then the logs are rolled into water and ground into chips. Chemicals are added, and the chips become pulp. The pulp is poured onto a moving screen. Water drains out of the pulp. A thin sheet of fibers is left. This sheet is heated and dried. Then it passes through rollers. At last it is paper!

1. Put these events in the order that they happened. What happened first? Write the number **1** on the line by that sentence. Then write the number **2** by the sentence that tells what happened next.

_____ Large numbers of books could be made.

_____ The printing press was invented.

_____ **2.** When was paper invented?
   A. in the 1400s
   B. 100 years ago
   C. before the printing press

_____ **3.** When is the bark cut off the logs?
   A. before the logs are rolled into water
   B. after the chemicals are added
   C. when a thin sheet of fibers is left

_____ **4.** When is the pulp poured onto a moving screen?
   A. when the sheet passes through rollers
   B. after the chips become pulp
   C. before egg cartons are recycled

Writing Roundup

Read the story below. Think about the sequence, or time order. Answer the questions in complete sentences.

Asha and Keisha went to the pond. They found some frog eggs. They took some home with pond water and pond weed. They put them into a fish tank. After a week, the eggs started to hatch. "Look!" said Asha. "They're tadpoles!" The tadpoles grew quickly. In seven weeks, they grew back legs. Then they grew front legs. Their tails got shorter. The tadpoles looked more and more like frogs. Their tails went away. The tadpoles had turned into frogs! Asha and Keisha took the frogs to the pond.

1. When did the frog eggs start to hatch?

_____

_____

2. When did the tadpoles grow back legs?

_____

_____

3. When did the tadpoles grow front legs?

_____

_____

Prewriting

Think about something that you have done, such as making a sandwich, setting up a tent, or making your bed. Write the events in sequence below.

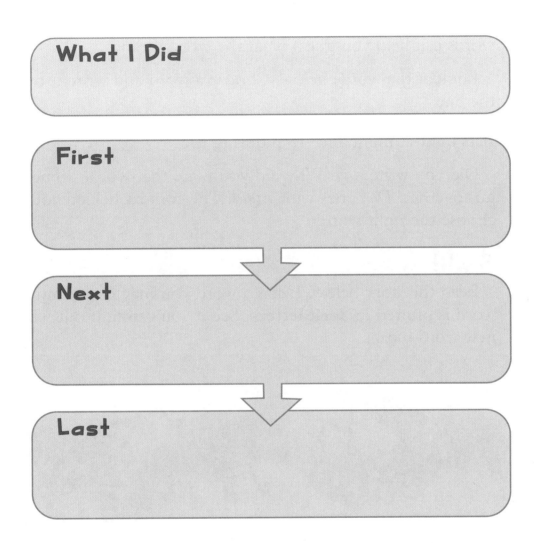

What I Did

First

Next

Last

On Your Own

Now use another sheet of paper to write a story about what you have done. Write the events in the order that they happened. Use time order words.

What Is Context?

You can use context to learn new words. If you find a word you do not know, look at the words around it. These other words can help you guess what the word means.

Look at the words below. Choose a word and write it on the line.

Bats hunt at night and sleep during the _____.

Did you write *day*? Why did you write that word? Some words go together. *Day* goes with *night*. The context helped you choose the right word.

Try It!

Read the story below. It has a word you may not know. The word is printed in **dark letters**. See if you can find out what the new word means.

Chuck Berry Makes a Hit

The singer named Muddy Waters listened to the young man. He really liked to hear him sing. He **encouraged** Chuck to make a record. "You're really good!" he said. "Go ahead and try to make the big time." Chuck's first record had a new kind of music. It was called rock and roll. Today many people say that Chuck Berry is the father of rock and roll.

How to Use Context

If you don't know what **encouraged** means, look at the context. Remember, the context is all the other words in the story. Here are some of the other words in the story. They can help you find out what **encouraged** means.

1. "You're really good!"

2. "Go ahead and try to make the big time."

Find these words in the story about Chuck Berry. Draw a circle around them. What words do you think of when you read the clues? Write a few words on the line below:

_____

Did you write a word like *help*? To *encourage* someone is to *help* someone by what you say or do.

• To use context, read all the words in a story. If some words are too hard, don't stop reading! Read all the words you can. They may tell you something about the words you could not read.

• When you try to find out what new words mean, remember that some words go together. Think of a meaning that goes with the other words in the story.

Read the stories in this unit. If a word in a story is missing, choose the word that fits. If there is a word in **dark letters** in a story, figure out what that word means.

Read each passage. After each passage you will answer a question about context. Remember, context is a way to learn new words by thinking about the other words used in a story.

Juan Largo has spent seven years learning about black bears. He catches the bears. Then he puts little radios on them. He can track the bears and __1__ down what they do. He even knows where they sleep during the winter. Sometimes he puts a tag on a bear's ear. Then he will know that bear when he sees it again.

_____ **1.** The word that best completes the sentence is

     A. back   **B.** write   **C.** sing

Many good baseball games have been played during the World Series. But one game had the fans on the edge of their seats. It was when the Yankees played the Dodgers. Don Larsen pitched a perfect game for the Yankees. No one on the Dodgers team ever hit the ball. No one got a walk, either. Not __2__ Dodger got on base! Of course the Yankees won the game.

_____ **2.** The word that best completes the sentence is

     A. on   **B.** working   **C.** one

Mangrove trees grow in salt water. Most trees take in water with their roots. Then they let it out through their leaves. When mangroves take in water, they take in salt, too. They let the water and the salt out. After that, mangroves look as if someone __3__ salt all over their leaves.

_____ **3.** The word that best completes the sentence is

     A. threw   **B.** liked   **C.** grew

A newt hatches from an egg under water. This small animal first lives in water. Later in life the newt grows lungs and moves to land. At this stage the newt is bright orange. Other animals can see it easily. But they do not __4__ it. They know that the newt's skin will make them sick.

_____ **4.** The word that best completes the sentence is

     A. bother   **B.** drive   **C.** iron

A beam of light from the Sun looks as if it's white. But it's really made up of many colors. These are the same colors you see in a __5__ after a storm. Light that goes from the Sun to Earth passes through the air first. Some light bounces off bits of dust in the air. The blue and purple beams in the light are the shortest and bounce the most. They bounce all over the sky. This is why the sky looks blue most of the time.

_____ **5.** The word that best completes the sentence is

     A. cup   **B.** rainbow   **C.** face

Scuba divers swim deep in the ocean. They use face masks to see better. They wear fins on their feet to help them swim. To breathe underwater, divers use air tanks. One or two tanks are __6__ onto their backs. Then divers can stay underwater for a long time. If the water is cold, they can wear wet suits to stay warm.

_____ **6.** The word that best completes the sentence is

     A. imagined   **B.** lost   **C.** strapped

At first Sandra was a lawyer. Later she worked as a judge. The president looked at Sandra's work. He saw that she treated people ___1___ in her court. He asked her to be a judge on the Supreme Court. Sandra Day O'Connor is the first woman ever to hold this job.

_____ 1. The word that best completes the sentence is

    A. poorly   **B.** fairly   **C.** wrongly

A ladybug is a type of small beetle. It has a small, round body. It looks like half of a pea. The ladybug is bright red or yellow. It has black, yellow, red, or white spots on its back. People who grow fruit like this bug. It is helpful. It eats other insects that harm fruit ___2___ .

_____ 2. The word that best completes the sentence is

    A. crops   **B.** clouds   **C.** games

A river made a ___3___ in Colorado. It's called Royal Gorge. People used to go through it to get to silver mines. Some people wanted to build a railroad through the deep valley. Two groups of people began to fight. Both of them wanted to build the railroad. Then one group sold out to the other. The railroad was finished.

_____ 3. The word that best completes the sentence is

    A. fan   **B.** canyon   **C.** window

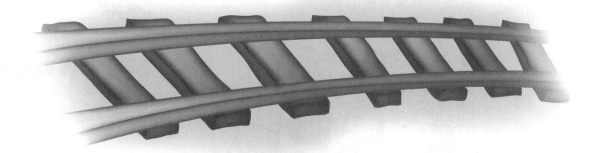

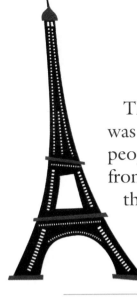

There was once a big fair in France. The Eiffel Tower was built for it. This tall tower was made of iron. Today people come from all over to see it. There is a great view from the top. You can even eat in a __4__ while you enjoy the view.

_____4. The word that best completes the sentence is
A. restaurant   B. book   C. garage

The Inuit people live in the far North. Life has changed for them through the years. Most Inuit once lived by the sea. In the summer they lived in tents. The tents were made of animal skins. In the __5__ they moved to new homes. They were made from blocks of dirt or ice. Now most Inuit live in towns.

_____ 5. The word that best completes the sentence is
A. water   B. afternoon   C. winter

You might have heard a cat purr when it came up to __6__ you. But have you ever wondered how it can make that sound? A cat purrs as it breathes in and out. When the air goes to and from the lungs, it passes through the cat's voice box. The cat can make the space in its voice box smaller. That changes the flow of air. The sound this makes is the cat's purr.

_____ 6. The word that best completes the sentence is
A. hold   B. greet   C. feed

The scorpion can be found in warm ___1___. It's a small animal. It has four pairs of legs. The scorpion has two large claws in front. It grabs and crushes its food with these claws. The scorpion has from six to twelve eyes. But it is best known for its tail. The scorpion stings with its tail. The sting is very painful, but it is usually not deadly.

_____ **1.** The word that best completes the sentence is

   A. shirts **B.** countries **C.** moons

There's a museum in Ohio. It's called the Cleveland Health Education Museum. People go there to learn how the human body works. There are huge models of an eye, an ear, and a tooth. The models are big enough for people to walk inside. People come from all over the ___2___ to see this museum.

_____ **2.** The word that best completes the sentence is

   A. turtle **B.** engine **C.** world

Light can pass through some objects, such as glass. You can see through these objects. But light can't pass through other objects. You cannot see through these. On the side of the object away from the source of light, there is a dark place on the ground. This shows where the light has been blocked. The dark spot is called a ___3___.

_____ **3.** The word that best completes the sentence is

   A. painting **B.** baby **C.** shadow

The day lily is a plant. It has __4__ without leaves. At the end of each one is a group of flowers. These flowers are yellow or orange. During the summer two or three of them bloom each day. They bloom when the Sun comes up. Then they die when the Sun sets.

_____ **4.** The word that best completes the sentence is
    A. fences   **B.** stalks   **C.** apartments

There's a museum where you can learn about the desert. You can see plants and animals that live in the desert. Snakes, bobcats, and elf owls are just a few of these animals. There are many kinds of __5__ plants. This museum is in an Arizona desert. It is called the Arizona-Sonora Desert Museum.

_____ **5.** The word that best completes the sentence is
    A. jolly   **B.** breakfast   **C.** cactus

A barnyard pig takes a bath in mud. This is not because it likes to be dirty. In fact it would like cool, clean water much better. But a pig must find a way to cool off. It can't __6__ to stay cool the way people do. So it will lie in the mud to stay cool. The thick mud also helps the pig's skin. Insects can't bite it, and the sun won't burn it.

_____ **6.** The word that best completes the sentence is
    A. fly   **B.** sweat   **C.** kick

Trees are important. People make many things from trees. Trees are also helpful. They hold the dirt in place and help make the air we breathe. Trees are also homes for many creatures. So we need to be sure we __1__ the trees. When old trees are cut down, new ones must be planted.

_____ **1.** The word that best completes the sentence is

    A. forget   **B.** find   **C.** save

A cat's tongue feels rough. This is true for all cats. House cats, lions, and tigers all have rough tongues. A cat uses its tongue in many ways. It __2__ itself to brush its fur. The cat removes dirt and loose hair this way. The cat also uses its rough tongue to scrape meat from a bone. When the cat is through, the bone is clean.

_____ **2.** The word that best completes the sentence is

    A. paints   **B.** licks   **C.** frightens

Young people can join the 4-H Club. The goal of this club is to improve head, heart, hands, and health. Members have a chance to learn skills. They also find out about careers. Members try out jobs by working on __3__ . These jobs may deal with plants, animals, food, or safety.

_____ **3.** The word that best completes the sentence is

    A. ice   **B.** moments   **C.** projects

Germs are living things. They are very small. They are so small that you need a microscope to see them. Germs can be found in all places. Many germs are harmless. Others can make you sick if they get inside your __4__. There are ways you can keep safe from these germs. Be sure to wash your hands, keep cuts clean, and stay away from someone who has a cold.

_____ **4.** The word that best completes the sentence is
    A. body   **B.** glasses   **C.** homework

Alvin is the name of a small ship. People use *Alvin* to study the sea. The ship goes under the water. The people ride inside of it. The deep sea is very dark, so *Alvin* has big headlights. They light up parts of the sea. Then __5__ take pictures. A long hook scoops up samples from the sea floor. Later, people study these pictures and samples.

_____ **5.** The word that best completes the sentence is
    A. cats   **B.** cameras   **C.** nails

The mimosa is a plant. It has parts that look like feathers. These parts are made from two rows of tiny leaves. When it rains, the leaves lie open. If an animal touches any of the leaves, they __6__ up. The leaves open again the next time it rains.

_____ **6.** The word that best completes the sentence is
    A. sit   **B.** fold   **C.** dress

Some snakes have four eyes. They have eyes that see in the day. They also have two more eyes. These eyes can see heat. Snakes use these eyes to look for food. A snake **gazes** all around with its special eyes. Its eyes cannot see a plant. Plants do not give off any heat. But the eyes can see a mouse. A mouse is warm and makes a good meal for a snake.

_____ **1.** In this story the word **gazes** means

    A. stares   **B.** gives   **C.** adds

Deep inside, Earth is made of very hot rock. The rock is so hot that it can turn water into steam. In some places this steam comes out of cracks in the ground. In other places people pipe the steam up from deep in the ground. People use this steam **energy** to warm their homes.

_____ **2.** In this story the word **energy** means

    A. ice   **B.** power   **C.** stream

What is vegetable art? Ask Bob Spohn. For 50 years Spohn has **whittled** faces and animals out of large vegetables. He uses a knife to make the faces. Then he paints them. He once made a smiling face from a giant pumpkin. The pumpkin was almost 1 yard high and weighed 110 pounds!

_____ **3.** In this story the word **whittled** means

    A. drawn   **B.** shaken   **C.** cut

How do desert animals get water? Some catch it on their bodies. Some snakes, lizards, and bugs sleep in the open air. Cool winds blow during the night. These winds take water from the desert air. By morning small drops of this water have landed on the bodies of the animals. They drink the water by licking it. The wind and the water are **necessary** for desert animals. Without the wind they might die.

_____ **4.** In this story the word **necessary** means

      A. thanked   **B.** pitched   **C.** needed

One bird really can swim like a fish. It is called the loon. This bird has been found more than 100 feet below the water's **surface**. The bird can also fly, but it cannot walk. Its legs are very far back on its body. When it tries to stand up, it falls over.

_____ **5.** In this story the word **surface** means

      A. hole   **B.** top   **C.** ribbon

Doctors did a study on how some people stay thin. They found that nervous people use more energy. They walk back and forth. They tap their toes. They drum their fingers. In one day these people burn up the energy it takes to run 5 miles. This finding may lead to a new kind of exercise. People may **squirm** the pounds away!

_____ **6.** In this story the word **squirm** means

      A. wiggle   **B.** jump   **C.** run

Not all sharks are mean. Nurse sharks look bad, but they almost never hurt people. Instead they stay on the bottom of the ocean. They swim along, **sucking** in sand, crabs, snails, and tiny fish. They spit out the sand and eat the animals!

_____ **1.** In this story the word **sucking** means

     A. rolling   **B.** pulling   **C.** calling

People have loved amber for thousands of years. Amber looks like stone, but it really comes from the gum of trees. This gum fell to the ground long ago. It was covered with dirt and then became hard. There it stayed until it was found. Pieces of amber can be **polished** to make beads and rings. To do this you must rub the amber for a very long time.

_____ **2.** In this story the word **polished** means

     A. shined   **B.** missed   **C.** hidden

Some farmers in China were digging a well. They dug deeper and deeper. Suddenly a shovel struck something hard. A farmer bent down and pushed the dirt away. He found himself looking into a person's eyes. The person was made of clay. Scientists later dug up the area. Under the earth were 3,000 clay **warriors**. Some were on horses. Many carried spears and knives. All of them were as big as real people.

_____ **3.** In this story the word **warriors** means

     A. fighters   **B.** pots   **C.** animals

The sap from a poison ivy plant causes itchy bumps on your skin. It is best to know what this plant looks like. Poison ivy grows as a vine or a shrub. The leaves are always in groups of three on each stem. The color, size, and shape of the leaves can be different for each plant. Poison ivy **blooms** in the first part of summer. It has small blossoms that turn into berries.

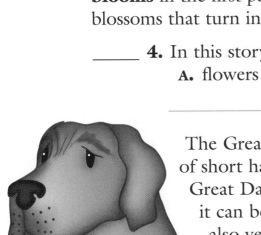

_____ **4.** In this story the word **blooms** means

  A. flowers **B.** cries **C.** travels

The Great Dane is a type of dog. It has a thick coat of short hair. Its hair can be black, tan, or white. The Great Dane is very large and strong. For this reason it can be used as a **guard** dog. But a Great Dane is also very gentle, so it makes a good pet, too.

_____ **5.** In this story the word **guard** means

  A. funny **B.** lazy **C.** watch

People wrote with secret codes long ago. Today many people still use secret codes. Two types of codes are used the most. In one kind of code, symbols take the place of letters. These symbols can be letters, numbers, or words. A code book is used to read the message. The other kind of code changes the **arrangement** of the letters. People must unscramble the letters to read the message.

_____ **6.** In this story the word **arrangement** means

  A. order **B.** shape **C.** face

The frostweed is a plant that grows in Texas. It grows best in the shade or in moist dirt. It is found under large trees and on the banks of creeks. This plant has a tall stem with a group of white flowers on the end. When the first freeze of the year comes, the plant's stem **splits**. Then sap leaks out. The sap freezes around the stem. It looks like ribbons or clusters of flowers.

_____ **1.** In this story the word **splits** means

      A. shuts   **B.** cracks   **C.** wanders

The first newspaper was a letter. It told the news. The letter was sent by messenger. It went to people who lived in far-off lands. Hundreds of years later, a news sheet was used. It was written by hand each day. Then it was **hung** up for all to read. Much later the Chinese carved wooden blocks. They printed a paper. Now the newspaper is a quick way to get the news.

_____ **2.** In this story the word **hung** means

      A. put   **B.** sawed   **C.** grown

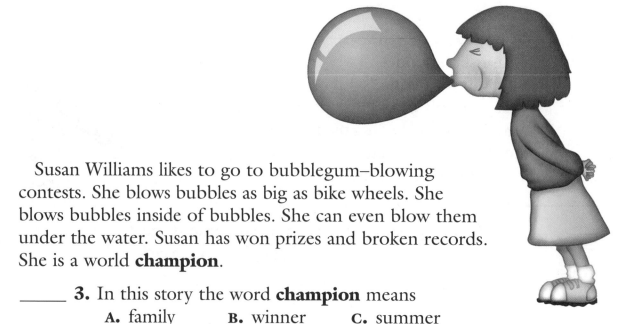

Susan Williams likes to go to bubblegum–blowing contests. She blows bubbles as big as bike wheels. She blows bubbles inside of bubbles. She can even blow them under the water. Susan has won prizes and broken records. She is a world **champion**.

_____ **3.** In this story the word **champion** means

      A. family   **B.** winner   **C.** summer

The *Mary Celeste* was a ship. It set sail more than 100 years ago. On board were the captain and a **crew** of eight sailors. One month after the *Mary Celeste* set sail, it was seen by another ship's captain. He saw that the *Mary Celeste* was going the wrong way. The captain went to find out what was wrong. He saw that no one was on board. He never found out what had happened to the people on the *Mary Celeste*.

_____ **4.** In this story the word **crew** means

      A. ladder   **B.** rock   **C.** team

A stinkbug is an insect. It can be green or brown. It can also be other colors. A stinkbug has a special trick. It uses its back legs or its stomach to make a bad smell. When the stinkbug gets scared, it can **spray** out the smelly liquid.

_____ **5.** In this story the word **spray** means

      A. splash   **B.** climb   **C.** find

The Big Dipper can be seen in the northern sky at night. It has seven stars. They form the **outline** of a pot. Three of the stars make the dipper's handle. Four of the stars make the rest of the pot. Two stars in the Big Dipper are brighter than the rest. They are called pointer stars. They can be used to find the North Star.

_____ **6.** In this story the word **outline** means

      A. shape   **B.** river   **C.** candle

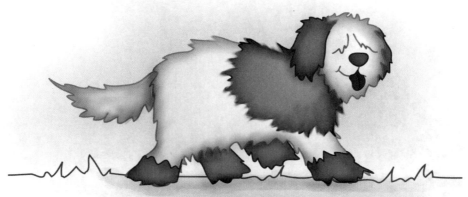

Some people think English sheepdogs make great pets. These dogs are cute and often friendly. They need much care. Their long, **shaggy** coats must be brushed every day. The dogs need lots of love and must have space in which to run.

_____ **1.** In this story the word **shaggy** means

    A. hairy   **B.** sorry   **C.** tiny

Roller coaster cars are hooked to a chain at first. A motor on the ground runs the chain. It pulls the cars to the top of the first hill. Then the cars are unhooked. When the cars roll downhill, they speed up. The cars slow down as they **coast** up the next hill. They speed up again as they go down it. Each hill is a bit lower than the last. The cars can't go up a hill that is as high as the one they just came down.

_____ **2.** In this story the word **coast** means

    A. move   **B.** park   **C.** leak

Stevie Wonder was blind from birth. This did not **prevent** him from using his talent. He found that he was good with music. He learned how to play many instruments. He wrote his own songs. At the age of 12, he sang his first hit. Since then he has made many recordings. He has even written music for movies.

_____ **3.** In this story the word **prevent** means

    A. help   **B.** take   **C.** stop

The Chicago River is in Illinois. It goes through the city of Chicago. People used to dump their **trash** into the river. This dirty water flowed to a nearby lake. Soon the lake water was dirty. Then the people found a way to keep the lake clean. They built dams on the river. The dams forced the water to flow away from the lake. Now the lake water stays clean.

_____ **4.** In this story the word **trash** means
      A. banana   **B.** garbage   **C.** sign

There's a special place in Michigan. It's a museum for children. The children come to learn about science. Some come from school. The museum sends a special truck for them. The children look at science **kits** during the ride. They look at rocks, models, and books.

_____ **5.** In this story the word **kits** means
      A. packages   **B.** organs   **C.** hills

Forest rangers watch for a fire in the woods. They try to stop a fire before it spreads. But this is not an easy job. Most fires start where the woods are thick. There aren't any roads in the middle of the woods, so firefighters can't drive to the fire. They must **parachute** from a plane to get there.

_____ **6.** In this story the word **parachute** means
      A. shoot   **B.** refuse   **C.** jump

Writing Roundup

Each of the sentences on this page is missing a word. Read the sentences. Choose a word from the word box to go in each one. Write the word on the line.

loud	feed	stood
leaves	glass	joke
wide	wear	true
afternoon	table	careful

1. It rained all _____.

2. The _____ on the trees turn red in the fall.

3. We _____ our pets every day.

4. Please pour me a _____ of milk.

5. Your funny _____ made me laugh.

6. That dog has a very _____ bark.

7. Please be _____ not to fall down.

8. It is _____ that all birds have feathers.

9. The puddle was too _____ to jump across.

10. We _____ in line to buy our tickets.

Read each story. Write a word on each line that makes sense in the story.

LaToya wanted to go outside. Snow was falling fast. "It looks **(1)**_____ in my front yard. Maybe I should put on my **(2)**_____," she said.

My dog Walter really likes to play with a **(3)**_____. I always hide it in the **(4)**_____. He uses his nose to find it. Then he brings it back to me.

The cow looked so funny! A yellow bird was sitting on its **(5)**_____! The cow switched its tail. Then the bird flew over to a **(6)**_____.

What Is a Main Idea?

The main idea of a story tells what the whole story is about. Each story in this book has a main idea. It is usually one sentence somewhere in each story.

Why do stories have sentences other than the main idea sentence? The other sentences are *details*. They tell you more about the main idea. They also make the story more fun to read.

The example below may help you think about main ideas. All the details add up to the main idea.

detail + detail + detail = main idea

3   +   4   +   5   =   12

The *3*, *4*, and *5* are like details. They add up to the main idea. The main idea is like the *12*. It is bigger than the details. It is made up of many smaller parts.

Try It!

Read the story below. Draw a line under the main idea.

Do you sing in the bathtub? Do you sing in the car? Here's how you can become a singing star! You can go to a store. Someone will play music while you sing a song. Then the people there will make a recording of your song. You can take it home and surprise your friends!

How to Choose a Main Idea

The main idea of the story is the sentence about becoming a singing star. All the other sentences are details. They tell how you can become a star. Write the details on the lines below.

Detail 1: You might sing in the _____
or in the _____.

Detail 2: You can go to a _____.

Detail 3: Someone will play _____.

Detail 4: The people will make a _____
of your song.

Detail 5: You can _____
your friends.

Now write the main idea on the lines below. It is the sentence that is not a detail.

Main Idea: _____

_____

- What do all the sentences add up to? Remember that the main idea is bigger than the details. It is made up of many smaller parts.

- Read each story. As you read, think about each sentence. Does it tell only a small part of the whole story? If it does, it is a detail. Does it tell what the story is about? Then it is the main idea.

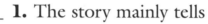

Lesson 1

Read each passage. After each passage you will answer a question about the main idea of the passage. Remember, the main idea is the main point in a story.

1. There's a lot of snow in some parts of the world. Schoolchildren in these places learn to make snowshoes. Snowshoes are big and flat. They are like duck feet. You put them on over your shoes. They are hard to walk in. But they keep your feet from sinking in the deep snow.

_____ **1.** The story mainly tells
- **A.** why snow falls
- **B.** why some children make snowshoes
- **C.** who wears duck feet in cold places

2. Newborn bats start life in a pocket. The mother bat makes her tail into a pocket. When a baby is born, the baby lives in it. The baby holds tight to its mother's fur. The mother hunts for food at night. The baby rides in its pocket. So baby bats get a free ride high in the sky each night.

_____ **2.** The story mainly tells
- **A.** why bats hold their mother's fur
- **B.** when to find bats in caves
- **C.** where baby bats live

3. What can you do if you're camping and you're caught in the rain without a tent? Rather than get wet, you can make a lean-to. First find two tree branches that are shaped like a Y. The branches should be tall and strong. Then put the two Y-shaped branches in the ground about eight feet apart. Next place a long, light stick across the two branches. Finally find many straight branches. Lean them against the cross stick on both sides. You will have a lean-to for sleeping and staying dry.

_____ **3.** The story mainly tells
    A. how to make a lean-to
    B. who needs a tent
    C. what to do if it rains

4. Have you seen any old trains? Most old trains were run by steam engine. The steam from the engine moved the train's wheels. The steam engine gave off puffs of smoke. The puffs came out of the train's smokestack. When the train ran fast, it gave off many puffs of smoke. A train going 50 miles per hour gave off 800 smoke puffs in a minute.

_____ **4.** The story mainly tells
    A. how trains stop
    B. about trains run by steam
    C. about train wheels

1. There's an old saying: "Sleep tight and don't let the bedbugs bite." But it's no joke. Bedbugs are real. They are small insects that eat blood. They bite animals and people, too. Their bites often hurt the skin. Bedbugs can be found hiding in beds and walls. If a bedbug does bite, a person probably won't sleep tight.

_____ **1.** The story mainly tells
   A. what bedbugs are like
   B. who gets bedbugs
   C. where bedbugs sleep

2. Read the story just before this one again. Try your best to remember it. Don't peek! How many sentences can you remember? Two? Three? None? Long ago, people told many stories. These people didn't know how to read or write, so they had to remember each story. Some stories were thousands of sentences long. How did they do it? They didn't try to remember every word. They just remembered how the story went. They told the story a little differently each time, too.

_____ **2.** The story mainly tells
   A. how many sentences you can remember
   B. who couldn't read or write
   C. how people long ago remembered stories

3. In the fall of each year, the days grow shorter and shorter. We finally reach a time when the days and nights last about the same number of hours and minutes. During these days the full moon is called a harvest moon. It rises soon after the Sun goes down. It is often a deep orange color. Since the Moon is so bright, farmers have more time to harvest their crops. That's why it's called a harvest moon.

_____ **3.** The story mainly tells
     A. what color the harvest moon is
     B. how the harvest moon got its name
     C. when the days grow shorter

---

4. The Statue of Liberty is one very big woman! Her hand is 16 feet long. One of her fingers is 8 feet long. Her head is 17 feet high. Her eyes are 2 feet wide. Even her fingernails are huge. They are more than 12 inches across.

_____ **4.** The story mainly tells
     A. how long some people's fingernails are
     B. how big the Statue of Liberty is
     C. who the tallest woman in the world is

1. Penguins are birds. But they cannot fly. They use their wings in other ways. They use them for swimming. Their wings are like flippers. In the summer they stay cool by holding their wings away from their bodies. Their wings are put to good use even if they cannot fly.

_____ **1.** The story mainly tells
   A. where penguins live
   B. how penguins use their wings
   C. how penguins stay warm

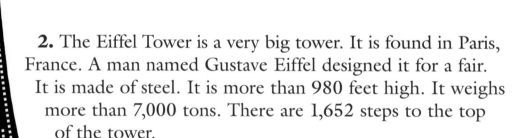

2. The Eiffel Tower is a very big tower. It is found in Paris, France. A man named Gustave Eiffel designed it for a fair. It is made of steel. It is more than 980 feet high. It weighs more than 7,000 tons. There are 1,652 steps to the top of the tower.

_____ **2.** The story mainly tells
   A. how big the Eiffel Tower is
   B. how many towers there are in France
   C. how the Eiffel Tower is used

3. A junk is a kind of boat. Junks sail on the seas of China and Southeast Asia. The sails of a junk have four sides. They are stretched over pieces of wood. Junks are used for fishing. Hong Kong is a very crowded city, so some people even live on their junks. A junk is sometimes a home for more than one family.

_____ **3.** The story mainly tells
  A. where most people in Hong Kong live
  B. about a boat called a junk
  C. what junks are made of

4. Emma Lazarus was a poet. She believed that America was the "land of the free." She knew that Jewish people were not treated fairly in many countries. She wanted to help them, so she wrote a poem. It is found on the Statue of Liberty. The statue and her famous poem greet the people who come to America.

_____ **4.** The story mainly tells
  A. that Lazarus built the Statue of Liberty
  B. that Lazarus didn't want to help people
  C. that Lazarus wrote about freedom

1. The white settlers thought bison were a kind of ox. Bison were hunted for their hides. The hides kept people warm. Bison meat made good food, too. The bison tongue was a special treat. Soon the big herds became small herds. Few bison were left. They were put on special land. Today bison live in protected herds.

_____ **1.** The story mainly tells
   A. about bison
   B. how bad bison tongue tasted
   C. that bison hides were not any good

2. Willie Mays loved baseball, but he couldn't play in the major leagues. African Americans couldn't play with white players. Mays played in the Negro Leagues. Then the New York Giants hired Mays. Mays played very well. He became a big star. He hit 660 home runs. Mays played with the Giants and the Mets. Today he is in the Baseball Hall of Fame.

_____ **2.** The story mainly tells
   A. how long Mays played baseball
   B. that Mays played for the Mets
   C. that Mays was a great baseball player

3. The fruit of the squirting cucumber looks like a little pickle. Its skin stretches as it grows. Pressure builds inside the fruit. When the fruit is ripe, it falls off the stem. This opens a hole at one end. The seeds squirt out from the hole. They can fly as far as 25 feet!

_____ **3.** The story mainly tells
 A. about a fruit that squirts its seeds
 B. about a kind of pickle
 C. where cucumber seeds come from

---

4. Fred Morrison invented the Frisbee. He wanted to make a pie tin into a toy. His first metal toy was too heavy. It didn't fly well, so he tried plastic. It sailed through the air. He sold the toy to a company that named it Pluto Platter. Later people played a game called Frisbie-ing. They threw pie tins from the Frisbie Pie Company. The toy company liked the game. It changed the spelling and called the toy a Frisbee.

_____ **4.** The story mainly tells
 A. how to spell Frisbee
 B. that Frisbee was fun to play
 C. how the Frisbee was invented

1. The first person went up into space in 1961. His name was Yuri Gagarin. He was Russian. His spacecraft was the *Vostok 1*. It circled Earth just one time. Gagarin was in space for less than two hours.

_____ **1.** The story mainly tells

     A. about the first manned spaceflight

     B. that *Vostok 1* was a planet

     C. which American was first in space

---

2. How are a toad and a frog different? A toad spends more time out of water than a frog does. A toad's skin is duller, rougher, and drier. The legs of a toad are shorter, too. A toad cannot jump as far as a frog can. A frog lays its eggs in a jelly-like mass. A toad lays its eggs in strings. It wraps the eggs around the stems of water plants.

_____ **2.** The story mainly tells

     A. where a frog lays its eggs

     B. how a frog and a toad are different

     C. how far a toad can jump

3. Sitting Bull was a Sioux leader. He didn't want his people to lose their land. He told the tribes to join against the white settlers. That way they might keep their homeland. In 1876, some tribes camped near the Little Bighorn River. General Custer and his troops charged the group. Sitting Bull's men destroyed the troops. It was a great win for Native Americans.

_____ **3.** The story mainly tells
  A. how Custer won the Battle of the Little Bighorn
  B. that Sitting Bull was a peaceful man
  C. how Sitting Bull's words helped the Sioux

---

4. The kiwi is a strange bird. It lives in New Zealand. The kiwi has tiny wings, but it cannot fly. It is covered with feathers that look like hair. Its bill is 6 inches long. Its nostrils are found at the end of its bill. It uses its bill to smell worms in the soil. The kiwi comes out only at night. It lives in holes near the roots of trees.

_____ **4.** The story mainly tells
  A. about the kiwi bird
  B. that a kiwi does not have feathers
  C. how far a kiwi can fly

1. Did you know that the world's largest bird can't fly? Can you name the bird? It's an ostrich. Why can't it fly? It's too big. An ostrich can be more than 8 feet tall. It can weigh more than 330 pounds. It lives in the grasslands of Africa.

_____ **1.** The story mainly tells
   A. which zoos have ostriches
   B. about the largest bird in the world
   C. how well ostriches hunt

---

2. How fast does the human heart beat? In most people, the heart beats 70 times per minute. A heart rate of 50 beats per minute is normal. So is a heart rate of 100. A healthy heart beats between 50 and 100 times a minute. A heart beats about three billion times in a lifetime!

_____ **2.** The story mainly tells
   A. about normal heart rates for humans
   B. how to measure your heartbeat
   C. about the heart rate during a heart attack

3. There are eight notes on a musical scale. Each scale starts and ends with the same letter. One scale is *C, D, E, F, G, A, B, C.* From one *C* to the next *C* is called an octave. *Octave* comes from the Greek word *okto* meaning "eight."

_____ **3.** The story mainly tells
   A. what a *C* note is
   B. how many scales there are
   C. what an octave is

4. Many babies were born at home in 1893. Esther Cleveland was born at home in that year. Her home was famous. It was the White House. Her father was President Grover Cleveland. Until that time, no other child of a president had been born in the White House.

_____ **4.** The story mainly tells
   A. how Cleveland was elected
   B. when Esther Cleveland was born
   C. about a baby born in the White House

1. Peeling an onion can make your eyes water. People try many things to keep from crying. Some people hold an onion under running water. Others try wearing goggles. Goggles make the cook look silly!

_____ **1.** The story mainly tells
- **A.** why onions make people cry
- **B.** ways to peel an onion without crying
- **C.** ways to use goggles

2. The thigh bone is the biggest bone in the body. It connects the hip bone to the knee bone. Why does it need to be big and strong? It has to support the weight of the body. It must hold up the leg muscles, too. It needs to be long so that the legs can take wide steps.

_____ **2.** The story mainly tells
- **A.** that the biggest bone is found in the arm
- **B.** why the thigh bone is so big
- **C.** how bones help a person walk

3. Many years ago, a company made a new tape. It was called Scotch tape. It was meant for use with clear wrapping. But some found other uses for the tape. They used it to mend old toys and torn clothing. They used it for many things. Later many companies made the same type of clear tape. They gave it new names. People bought these new tapes, but the first name given to the clear tape stuck. So now when people use clear tape, they call it Scotch tape.

_____ **3.** The story mainly tells
   A. how clear tape works
   B. why old toys are taped
   C. why clear tapes are called Scotch tape

4. Do you like yo-yos? Where do you think they started? Some people think that the yo-yo began in the United States, but the first yo-yo came to the United States in 1929. It came from the Philippines. The word *yo-yo* means "come come" in the Filipino language.

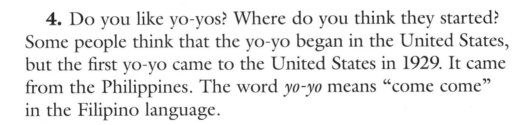

_____ **4.** The story mainly tells
   A. where the yo-yo started
   B. that the yo-yo was invented in 1939
   C. how to say *come* in the Filipino language

1. Sometimes people can't remember their dreams, but everyone dreams while sleeping. Most people dream two hours every night. In that time they have four or five dreams. Each dream is longer than the dream before. You can tell when someone is dreaming. Their eyeballs move back and forth under their closed eyelids.

_____ **1.** The story mainly tells
- **A.** how much sleep people need
- **B.** how often people dream
- **C.** what dreams mean

2. In 1904, New York opened its subway for train travel in the city. The fast trains took 28 minutes. They went from one end of the city to the other. Some trains made more stops. They took 46 minutes. It cost 5¢ to ride the train. People loved the ride and the price.

_____ **2.** The story mainly tells
- **A.** how to travel in New York
- **B.** about the 1904 New York subway
- **C.** when the subway made stops

3. Do you like bananas? Have you ever seen them growing outside? Bananas grow in bunches. A bunch of bananas is called a hand. Bananas grow in big hands. Each banana is called a finger. Each finger grows upward.

_____ **3.** The story mainly tells
  A. how bananas grow
  B. how to eat bananas with your fingers
  C. how the banana got its name

4. A snake doesn't open its mouth to stick out its tongue. The snake's jaw has a notch that lets the tongue move in and out. The tongue is not poisonous. A snake uses its tongue to smell. The tongue picks up air and carries it back into the mouth. There are two small holes on the roof of the mouth. It is these holes that smell the air.

_____ **4.** The story mainly tells
  A. how a snake uses its tongue to smell
  B. that a snake's tongue is poisonous
  C. that a snake has three holes on its tongue

Writing Roundup

Read each story. Think about the main idea. Write the main idea in your own words.

1. In 1987, an 18-month-old girl fell into a well in her yard. Her name was Jessica McClure. She was trapped there. People worked to save her. It took more than two days, but she was pulled free. Jessica was lucky to be alive!

What is the main idea of this story?

_____

_____

2. We think of the White House as the home of the president, but this was not always true. George Washington did not live in the White House. He lived in New York.

What is the main idea of this story?

_____

_____

3. Gail Devers won a gold medal in the 1992 Olympic Games. She was one of the fastest women in the world. She had come a long way. Her high school had no track team or coach. So Gail had to train herself.

What is the main idea of this story?

_____

_____

Prewriting

Think of a main idea that you would like to write about, such as a family member, a hero, or a place to go. Fill in the chart below.

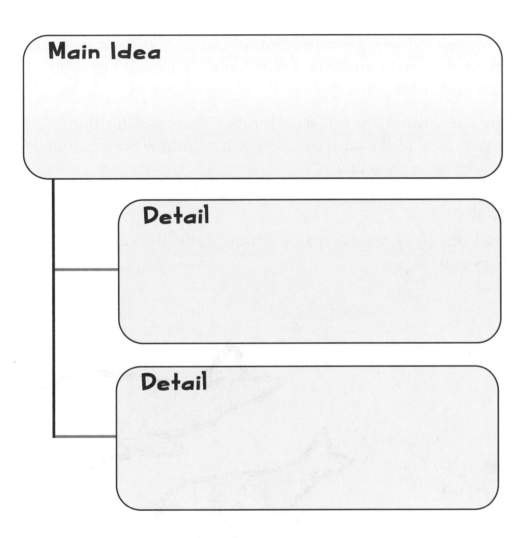

Main Idea

Detail

Detail

On Your Own

Now use another sheet of paper to write your story. Underline the sentence that tells the main idea.

What Is a Conclusion?

A conclusion is a decision you make after thinking about all the clues. A writer does not always tell you his or her conclusions. When you read, you have to hunt for clues. Then you must put all the clues together to draw a conclusion. This will help you understand the story.

The conclusions are not stated in the stories of this unit. You will have to read the stories. Then you will draw conclusions from what you have read.

Try It!

Read this story about whales. Think about the clues it gives you.

A mother whale helps her baby take its first breath. She pushes the new baby up for air. The mother whale stays by her baby for about a year. She keeps the baby safe. She feeds it milk.

How to Draw a Conclusion

Look at the story about whales again. Look at the clues in the story. They will help you draw a conclusion about mother whales. Write the clues about mother whales on the lines. The first one has been done for you.

Clue 1: A mother whale _helps her baby take its_
first breath. .

Clue 2: A mother whale _____
_____ .

Clue 3: A mother whale _____
_____ .

Now try to draw a conclusion about whales. Do you think that whales take care of their babies?

Conclusion: Whales take _____
_____ .

- Look at all the clues in the story. The first clue about the mother whale is that she helps her baby take its first breath. A second clue is that she keeps her baby safe. A third clue is that she feeds her baby milk.

- Look at all the clues together. If it helps, write the clues in your own words. Then make a decision about the story. Your decision will come from the clues. From the story about whales, you might decide that mother whales care for their babies. How do you know that? Mother whales help their babies breathe. They also give them safety and food.

Read each passage. After each passage you will answer a question that will require you to draw a conclusion about the story. Remember, a conclusion is a decision you make after putting together all the clues you are given.

1. When the whistle blows, everyone gets off the ice. The ice is bumpy and rough. Sharp skates have made cuts in it. A noisy machine moves around the rink like a fat duck. The machine makes the ice as smooth as glass. The machine was first built in California in 1942. Before 1942, it took two hours to smooth the ice. Three people did the job with shovels.

_____ **1.** From this story you can tell
    A. the machine makes a hard job much easier
    B. four people can work as fast as the machine
    C. three people push the machine on the ice

2. In Israel hundreds of people live together on a *kibbutz*. A kibbutz is a very large farm. Most of the people are farmers. Some are doctors, soldiers, or teachers. They all share the work. Everyone decides which crops to grow. The children live together in a special house. They see their parents only at night or on weekends.

_____ **2.** From this story you can tell
    A. people grow apples on the farms
    B. the children never play with other children
    C. a kibbutz is a special kind of farm

3. Without the Sun nothing could live on Earth. It would be too cold. But the Sun won't last forever. Millions of years from now, the Sun will stop shining. It will run out of gases to burn. When this happens, the Sun will become very big. It will burn brightly for a short time. Then it will cool and become very small.

_____ **3.** From this story you can tell
  A. when the Sun cools, it will become big
  B. after the Sun dies, Earth will die
  C. someday the Sun will turn bright blue

4. George Goodale loved plants. He wanted to have some plants in his museum, but he didn't want just any old plants. Dried plants wouldn't look very nice. Wax plants would melt. Live plants would need too much care. So he used glass plants. Today, people can look at them in his museum. The berries look good enough to eat. The cactus plants have spines that look real. Each glass spine was made by hand.

_____ **4.** From this story you can tell
  A. glass plants look nicer than dried plants
  B. glass plants change colors in the sun
  C. wax plants look as nice as glass plants

1. There are bugs that live under the ground for 17 years. As young bugs they spend their time eating roots. Finally in their seventeenth summer, they crawl up into the open air. They climb the trees and live for just a few weeks. Then they die. Everybody knows when these bugs come out. The males sing to their mates all day long. Sometimes their sound can even drown out airplane noise.

_____ **1.** From this story you can tell
   A. these bugs bite people
   B. the males sing only at night
   C. the bugs' sound is very loud

2. Did you know that your eyes bend light? When light enters the eyes, it's bent into a narrow band. This band of light lands on the back part of the eyes. The band must be bent just the right amount. If it isn't bent enough, things look fuzzy. If the world looks fuzzy, you may need eyeglasses. Eyeglasses can help your eyes see things more clearly.

_____ **2.** From this story you can tell
   A. things always look fuzzy when it's dark
   B. eyeglasses help people's eyes bend light
   C. eyeglasses come in many different colors

3. "Cooking is easy," Lisa said. "Who needs lessons? I know what to do." Lisa turned the stove on high. She put the ham over the hot flame. Jenny put some salt into the tea. Then she added water and let it boil. The girls also decided to make some bread. "What about all the lumps?" Lisa asked. Jenny said, "Just hope that nobody notices, I guess." By now the ham had burned. The tea tasted awful, too. So Lisa and Jenny had peanut butter sandwiches for dinner!

_____ **3.** From this story you can tell
> **A.** the girls really need cooking lessons
> **B.** the girls have cooked for many years
> **C.** the girls tried to bake a cake

---

4. Tara had to walk through a strange part of the city. She hid her necklace inside her shirt so that it wouldn't show. Her money was in her bag. She held the bag close to her body. She had a whistle in her hand. Tara held her head high and walked fast.

_____ **4.** From this story you can tell
> **A.** Tara worked for a big company in the city
> **B.** Tara was afraid of being robbed or hurt
> **C.** Tara had many necklaces

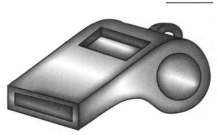

1. There is a man who makes music by playing glasses of water. He buys plain glasses at the store. Then he puts them on a table and fills them with water. He fills some glasses full. He fills others halfway. He pours just a little water in the rest of the glasses. Then he plays music by running his wet finger around the tops of the glasses. He changes the sounds by adding water or pouring water out of the glasses.

_____ **1.** From this story you can tell
   A. this man really likes to play the harp
   B. the amount of water changes the sound
   C. the man uses 15 glasses to play a song

2. Who began the idea of birthday parties? About 800 years ago, the Germans had the first birthday party. It was held on a child's birthday. The party began when the child awakened. There were candles on the birthday cake. The candles were kept lit all day long. There was also a big dinner. After the meal the child blew out the candles. Then everyone ate some birthday cake.

_____ **2.** From this story you can tell
   A. the cake was eaten in the morning
   B. the candles were blown out in the evening
   C. the candles were lit after the big meal

3. People have eaten popcorn for thousands of years. Native Americans were among the first to eat this snack. Not all corn will pop. A kernel of corn must have water in it to pop. When the water in the corn is heated, it turns to steam. The steam makes the kernels pop into puffs.

_____ **3.** From this story you can tell
  A. popcorn is a very old snack
  B. all corn is used as popcorn
  C. popcorn was first eaten at a movie.

4. Two-thirds of Earth is covered with water. There are many oceans and seas. The Pacific Ocean is the biggest one. It covers more than 60 million square miles. This is about one-third of Earth's surface. This ocean holds half the world's water. Some parts of the Pacific are more than six miles deep.

_____ **4.** From this story you can tell
  A. the Pacific Ocean is bigger than Earth
  B. Earth's surface has more water than land
  C. the Pacific Ocean is not very deep

1. Have you ever looked at a map of the United States? Many states have strange shapes. The bottom part of Michigan looks like a mitten. Maine looks like the head of a buffalo. Tennessee is shaped like a sled. Also, California looks like an arm. Try to remember these strange shapes. They will help you remember the states.

_____ **1.** From this story you can tell
   A. many states have different shapes
   B. Maine has the shape of a mitten
   C. the shapes will help you forget the states

---

2. In Europe most people eat with the fork held in the left hand. Most Americans hold it in their right hand. Why is it different? In the pioneer days, there was not always enough food to eat. So people ate very fast. They could eat even faster by holding the fork in their right hand.

_____ **2.** From this story you can tell
   A. pioneers liked to eat slowly
   B. everyone holds the fork in his or her left hand
   C. Americans and Europeans eat differently

3. An old fairy tale tells of Goldilocks and the three bears. At first, it was not about a young girl. Instead, it was about an old woman with gray hair. Her name was Silver Hair. The story was told through the years. Some people changed the old woman to a young girl. They called her "Golden Hair." Later she was called "Goldilocks."

_____ **3.** From this story you can tell
    A. the story of Goldilocks has changed
    B. an old woman wrote the story of Goldilocks
    C. Goldilocks is an old German tale

4. In 1991, Richard Branson and Per Lindstrand did a brave thing. They flew across the Pacific Ocean. They did not fly in a jet. They crossed the ocean in a hot-air balloon! They were the first people to do this. They floated from Japan to Canada. Their trip covered more than 6,000 miles.

_____ **4.** From this story you can tell
    A. the balloon trip was not very long
    B. the men traveled very far
    C. the balloon trip ended in Japan

1. Today you can find buttons on many clothes, but buttons have not always been used to fasten clothes. Long ago only belts and pins were used to join parts of clothes. For hundreds of years, buttons were used as jewels. They were put on clothes just for their beauty. Finally in the 1200s, buttons were used as fasteners on clothes.

_____ **1.** From this story you can tell
   A. buttons are still used only for beauty
   B. pins and belts are better than buttons
   C. buttons, belts, and pins are used as fasteners

2. Marco Polo was a famous traveler. His home was in Venice, Italy. In 1271, he made a trip to the Far East. In China he became friends with the ruler. His name was Kublai Khan. Polo became his helper. He stayed in China for 20 years. Then he went back home. There he wrote a book. The book told all about the Far East.

_____ **2.** From this story you can tell
   A. Polo got lost on his trip
   B. Venice is west of China
   C. Polo did not stay long in China

3. Have you ever seen someone turn a thumbs up? Today a thumbs up means good luck. The early Egyptians used a thumbs up to mean hope. They also used it to mean winning. To them a thumbs down meant losing or bad luck.

_____ **3.** From this story you can tell
- **A.** a thumbs up means bad luck
- **B.** a thumbs down means winning
- **C.** a thumbs up means good things

---

4. The biggest cave room in the world is called the Big Room. It is found at Carlsbad Caverns in New Mexico. The edge of the Big Room is almost 2 miles around. Its floor covers 14 acres. This is bigger than 12 football fields put together. Its roof is more than 300 feet tall. A building with 30 floors could fit into the Big Room!

_____ **4.** From this story you can tell
- **A.** this cave room has the right name
- **B.** Carlsbad Caverns is a hotel
- **C.** the Big Room is found in New Jersey

1. Alan Shepard Jr. became famous on May 5, 1961. He was strapped to his seat inside a spaceship. The spaceship was named *Freedom 7.* All of a sudden, the ship started to shake. Its great engines roared. Then Shepard raced through the sky. Soon he reached space. His trip took only 15 minutes. He was the first American to fly in space.

_____ **1.** From this story you can tell
  A. Shepard flew to Mars
  B. Shepard's trip into space was short
  C. Shepard rode a balloon into space

2. The man who first made chewing gum was named Thomas Adams. He was really trying to make rubber, not gum. He used something called chicle. Chicle is the sticky sap from a Mexican tree. Adams was not able to make rubber from chicle. He got his money back and he sold the chicle as chewing gum!

_____ **2.** From this story you can tell
  A. chewing gum comes from trees
  B. chicle is a kind of small chicken
  C. chewing gum is now made from rubber

3. Have you ever read *Roll of Thunder, Hear My Cry*? It is a book by Mildred D. Taylor. It is told through the eyes of Cassie Logan. Cassie is a smart girl. She is nine years old. Cassie learns of the pride her family has in its roots. In this book and in others, Taylor tells wonderful stories of earlier African American life.

_____ **3.** From this story you can tell
   A. Cassie Logan is afraid of thunder
   B. Mildred D. Taylor is an African American
   C. Cassie learns about her family's roots

G. Washington   T. Jefferson   J. Madison   J. Monroe   W. H. Harrison   J. Tyler   Z. Taylor   W. Wilson

4. Virginia is part of the United States. It is known as the Mother of Presidents. Eight presidents were born in this state. More presidents have come from Virginia than from any other state. George Washington was the first president born there. Thomas Jefferson was another. James Madison, James Monroe, and William Henry Harrison were next. Then came John Tyler and Zachary Taylor. Woodrow Wilson was the last president from Virginia.

_____ **4.** From this story you can tell
   A. Virginia is really eight states put together
   B. many presidents have been born in Virginia
   C. Washington's mother was born in Virginia

1. Some towns in the United States have strange names. Many of these names are not English. Take Baton Rouge as an example. It's the capital of Louisiana. Its name comes from French words. *Baton rouge* means "red stick." Long ago, Native Americans used red sticks to mark off their hunting grounds. The French settlers named the town after these red sticks.

_____ **1.** From this story you can tell
     A. the names of towns are not always English
     B. Baton Rouge is a French settler's name
     C. Louisiana is part of England

2. There are different ways to tell how hot or cold it is outside. Do you know a fun way to measure the heat? First you must listen for the cricket chirps. Then you need to count the chirps for 15 seconds. Then add 40 to the number of chirps. Your answer should be close to the real temperature.

_____ **2.** From this story you can tell
     A. crickets chirp louder when it is cold
     B. only crickets are used to measure the heat
     C. crickets chirp faster as the heat rises

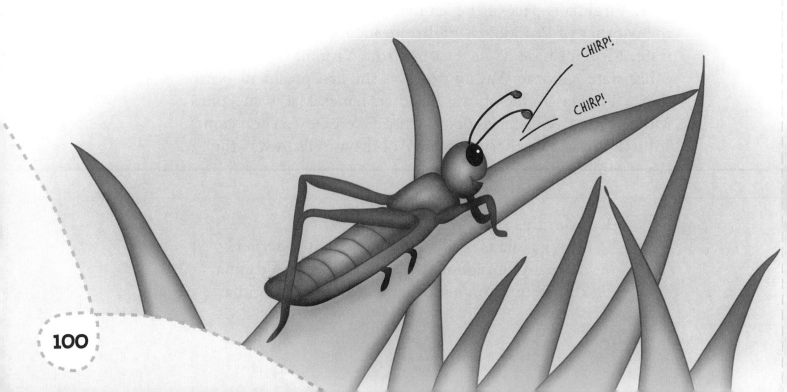

3. Charles Blondin was a brave man.
In 1859, he crossed Niagara Falls on a tightrope.
Then he put on a blindfold and crossed the rushing water
again. But that wasn't all he did. He walked the rope with stilts.
As his last trick, he walked halfway across the tightrope. There he
stopped for breakfast! He cooked some eggs and ate them. Then
he made his way to the other side.

_____ **3.** From this story you can tell
      A. Blondin was a poor swimmer
      B. Blondin was comfortable on the tightrope
      C. Blondin was not afraid of water

4. Many states have nicknames. Alaska is the Great Land.
Texas is called the Lone Star State. Maine is known as the Pine
Tree State. Why do they have these nicknames? There are stories
behind them. One example is Wyoming. It's called the Equality
State. Wyoming became a state in 1890. Its laws gave women the
right to vote. It was the first state to do this for women.

_____ **4.** From this story you can tell
      A. Alaska has many pine trees
      B. Texas became a state in 1890
      C. Wyoming gave equal rights to women

1. An astronaut is someone who works in space. Ellen Ochoa is the first Hispanic woman astronaut. She does experiments in space. Some of the experiments help us know how the Sun works. This helps us see how the Sun affects Earth. In her spare time, she likes to play the flute. She rides her bike and plays volleyball, too.

_____ **1.** From this story you can tell
  A. Ellen Ochoa plays flute in a band
  B. Ellen Ochoa wins bike races
  C. Ellen Ochoa works in space

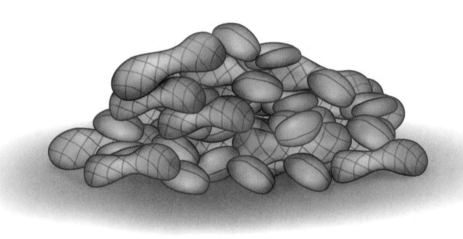

2. Do you like peanuts? Many people do. In fact, March is known as Peanut Month. People in the United States eat many peanuts. They eat more than 1 billion pounds of peanuts per year. Half of this is eaten as peanut butter.

_____ **2.** From this story you can tell
  A. peanuts are a favorite American snack
  B. May is Peanut Month
  C. peanut butter is made from walnuts

3. The year was 1960. Chubby Checker was only 19 years old. Checker liked to dance, but he was tired of the same old dances. He wanted a new dance. So he made up a few new steps. The dance was called the Twist. He even wrote a song to go along with his new dance. Soon young people everywhere were doing the Twist.

_____ **3.** From this story you can tell
  A. people did not like Checker's new song
  B. Checker never learned to dance
  C. the Twist became a well-known dance

---

4. The 1939 World's Fair was held in New York. One of the fun parts of the fair was called Futurama. It tried to show what the future might be like. It showed how people would one day use air conditioners. This idea became true. It also showed people living in houses that could be thrown away. This idea has yet to become real.

_____ **4.** From this story you can tell
  A. the World's Fair took place in New Jersey
  B. Futurama showed things from the past
  C. it's hard to tell about the future

Writing Roundup

Read each story. Think about a conclusion you can draw.
Write your conclusion in a complete sentence.

1. Dorothy Kelly became famous in 1977. The plane she
was on crashed into another plane. She helped to save many lives
during the accident. She thought she was only doing her job.
The airline thought she did more than she had to do.

What conclusion can you draw?

_____

_____

2. In basketball, you get points
when you make a basket. Some baskets
give you more points than others. These
baskets are not easy to make. They are
a big risk. That is why they are not tried
as often as other basketball shots.

What conclusion can you draw?

_____

_____

_____

3. Mrs. Paz opened the classroom. Then she pulled
up the blinds. Next she watered the plants. She put
the new books on the desks. The room was ready. The
girls and boys would be there soon. Mrs. Paz liked all
of them.

What conclusion can you draw?

_____

_____

_____

Read the story below. What conclusions can you draw? Use the clues in the story to answer the questions in complete sentences.

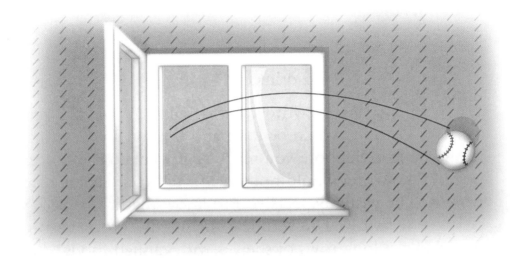

The living room window was open. Cody was not happy to see the open window. He had asked his little brother Tom to keep the window closed. Tom said that he needed more fresh air. All of a sudden, a baseball came sailing through the open window. It landed on the couch. Cody smiled at his little brother and Tom smiled back at him.

1. Who opened the window? How do you know?

_____

_____

2. Where was Cody? How do you know?

_____

_____

3. Was it good that the window was open? How do you know?

_____

_____

What Is an Inference?

An inference is a guess you make after thinking about what you already know. For example, a friend invites you to a party. From what you know about parties, you might infer that there will be games, gifts, food, and drinks.

An author does not write every detail in a story. If every detail were told, stories would be long and boring, and the main point would be lost. Suppose you read, "Pat went to the grocery store." The writer would not have to tell you what a grocery store is. The writer expects you to know that it is a place where people buy food. When you hear the words "grocery store," you may think of long rows of shelves with canned foods. You may think of cases filled with cheese and milk. By filling in these missing details, you could infer that Pat went to the store to buy food. The writer expects you to infer the missing details from what you know.

Try It!

Read this story about Sam.
Think about the facts in the story.

Sam's Morning

Sam walked down the hall at school. He pushed back his straight, red hair with one hand. He hadn't combed it. He rubbed his eyes with a fist. He hadn't washed his face. His shirt was wrinkled. One shoelace was untied. It dragged along the floor as he walked.

How to Make an Inference

Look at the story about Sam again. Look at the facts in the story. They will help you make an inference about Sam. Write the facts on the lines. The first one has been done for you.

Fact 1: Sam had forgotten <u>to comb his hair</u>.

Fact 2: He hadn't _____.

Fact 3: His shirt _____.

Fact 4: One shoelace _____.

Now try to make an inference about Sam. Do you think Sam cares about how he looks?

Inference: Sam _____.

- Look at all the facts in the story. Sam hadn't combed his hair. He hadn't washed his face. His shirt was wrinkled. One shoelace was not tied.

- Now go beyond what you've read. What can you guess about Sam? Your inference will come from what you read and what you already know. Did you guess that Sam doesn't care about how he looks? You can infer that because Sam hadn't combed his hair or washed his face. Also, his shirt was wrinkled, and his shoelace was not tied.

Read each passage. After you read each passage you will be asked to make an inference about the story. Remember, an inference is a guess you make by putting together what you know and what you read or see in the stories.

1. Manx cats come from an English island. It is the Isle of Man in the Irish Sea. Manx cats have short hair. Rumpy Manx cats have no tail at all. Stumpy Manx cats have short tails. Longie Manx cats have long tails. They all have short front legs and long back legs. They have short, round heads, faces, and bodies. Sometimes they hop. For that reason, people once thought they were part rabbit.

_____ **1.** Which of these sentences is probably true?
    A. Manx cats are part rabbit.
    B. Only cats live on the Isle of Man.
    C. Manx cats were named after the island.

2. The Blues moved the ball down the field. One player kicked it to another. The Reds could not take the ball away. The Blues got closer to the net. The Reds' goalie caught one of the balls that was kicked into the net. She did not catch the next one. The Blues scored still another point.

_____ **2.** Which of these sentences is probably true?
    A. The Blues were winning the game.
    B. The Reds needed more players.
    C. The Blues were sore losers.

3. The whooping crane is one of two kinds of cranes that live in North America. It is a large bird with a long neck and long legs. Long ago these cranes lived on the grasslands. Then people moved to these places. The people took the land where these cranes had made homes. The cranes began to disappear. At one point there were just 21 cranes left. Then people started to help these cranes. They gave them space to build nests. They helped keep the cranes safe.

_____ **3.** Which of these sentences is probably true?
   A. People found that the cranes needed help.
   B. People used whooping cranes for food.
   C. No whooping cranes are left today.

4. The Smithsonian is a big museum. The bones of animals that lived long ago are kept there. You can also see clothes, tools, and cars that people have used in the past. The first U.S. rocket is there, too.

_____ **4.** Which of these sentences is probably true?
   A. The Smithsonian sells cars.
   B. You can learn about the past at the Smithsonian.
   C. The Smithsonian has live animals.

1. Yin-May was driving on the road. She saw an airplane over her car. It was a warm day, and her windows were rolled down. Yin-May heard the plane's engine go off and then on. This happened many times. The plane turned and came in low over the road. The plane turned again. Yin-May pulled off the road.

_____ **1.** Which of these sentences is probably true?

   A. Yin-May was waiting for her mother.

   B. The plane had problems and needed to land.

   C. The pilot was counting the cars on the road.

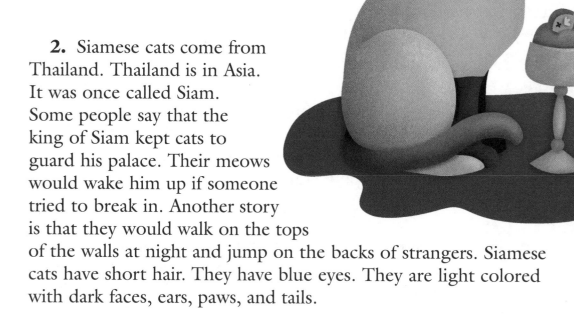

2. Siamese cats come from Thailand. Thailand is in Asia. It was once called Siam. Some people say that the king of Siam kept cats to guard his palace. Their meows would wake him up if someone tried to break in. Another story is that they would walk on the tops of the walls at night and jump on the backs of strangers. Siamese cats have short hair. They have blue eyes. They are light colored with dark faces, ears, paws, and tails.

_____ **2.** Which of these sentences is probably true?

   A. Siamese cats have blue faces.

   B. Siamese cats are afraid of the king.

   C. Siamese cats are loud.

3. The Tennessee River runs through high hills. For years the river flooded. Water ran over the banks of the river. The water ruined fields and houses. People built a high dam. Water collected behind the dam. This made a lake. When it rained, the floodwater went into the lake.

_____ **3.** Which of these sentences is probably true?
   A. The Tennessee River dried up.
   B. Dams help stop flooding.
   C. River water is not safe to drink.

4. Maria uses her new tools to build a bluebird house. She draws the shape of each side on a piece of cedar. She cuts the board with her hand saw. She nails each side to the floor. Then she nails on the roof. She uses a large drill to make a door for the birds. Her friend Suki helps her find a good place to hang the birdhouse. Now they wait for the bluebirds to move in and raise a family.

_____ **4.** Which of these sentences is probably true?
   A. Maria likes bluebirds.
   B. All birdhouses are made of cedar.
   C. Suki has new tools.

1. Oil is a resource. Coal and gas are also resources. They are all fuels. We burn these fuels to make heat and power. We use gas and oil to run our cars. All three of these resources come from the ground. They were formed long before people lived on Earth.

_____ **1.** Which of these sentences is probably true?
  A. No one uses resources.
  B. Oil, gas, and coal are not resources.
  C. Oil, coal, and gas help people to meet needs.

2. In the 1800s, a man from France wanted people all over the world to know that America stood for freedom. He asked an artist friend to help him. First the artist drew a picture of a woman wearing a long robe. He showed the woman holding a torch and wearing a crown. The statue was finished in 1886. Now it stands on Liberty Island. It has greeted many people who have come to America.

_____ **2.** Which of these sentences is probably true?
  A. The man's statue was never finished.
  B. The statue is the Statue of Liberty.
  C. The statue stands for all artists.

3. Even though she didn't speak, I knew Mom was mad. Her face was red. Her arms were crossed. She was standing in the doorway, tapping her foot. I was late again. I tried to run up to my room fast.

_____ **3.** Which of these sentences is probably true?
    A. Mom was pleased with me.
    B. People can say things without using words.
    C. Mom shouted, and I knew she was mad.

---

4. The two children lay on their backs in the grass. They were looking up at the sky. "I see a whale. See him spout!" said one. "That doesn't look like a whale," said the other. "It looks like an elephant." Neither could agree on the shapes they saw.

_____ **4.** Which of these sentences is probably true?
    A. The children were watching cartoons outside.
    B. An elephant was riding a whale.
    C. The children were seeing shapes in the clouds.

1. How is the air heated in a hot-air balloon? Pilots use a gas flame to heat the air. If a pilot wants to go up, he or she shoots the flame up into the balloon. This makes the air hot. The pilot must cool the air to go down. Once the balloon is up, the wind guides the balloon. If there is no wind, the balloon stays in one place.

_____ **1.** Which of these sentences is probably true?
    A. Hot air makes the balloon rise.
    B. Balloons get you places fast.
    C. Hot-air balloons fly with wings.

2. Some insects have built-in ways to hide from their enemies. One insect looks just like a stick. Its body is long, thin, and brown. Its legs are very thin. When birds see it, they think it is a twig, so they don't eat it. Another insect looks like a leaf. It is green and flat, and it hangs on a plant. Birds think it is part of the plant.

_____ **2.** Which of these sentences is probably true?
    A. Birds are not very smart.
    B. Some insects are shaped like parts of plants.
    C. Insects love to play tricks.

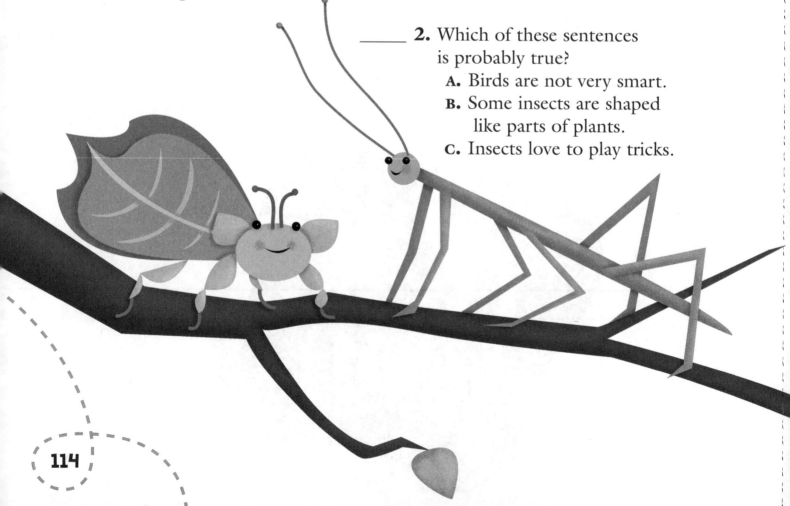

3. We put all the books away in boxes. The teacher took our little bits of crayon and threw them away. She put our big ones in a box. Some children took the pictures off the walls. I washed the chalkboard. The janitor came in to lock the windows. The teacher put her plants in a box to take home.

_____ **3.** Which of these sentences is probably true?
  A. It is the first day of school.
  B. It is the last day of school.
  C. There has been a fire at school.

4. Some words sound just alike. Sometimes this can cause trouble. Suppose someone asks you to pick up rocks with a crane. What should you do? Do you use a bird with a long neck? Or do you use a machine? How will you know which crane to use?

_____ **4.** Which of these sentences is probably true?
  A. Words can sound alike but have different meanings.
  B. _Crane_ and _crane_ do not sound the same.
  C. All words have the same meaning.

1. Jan counted out five pairs of socks. She put one extra pair in the pile. She found the T-shirt she liked to sleep in. She chose some shorts and shirts. "Don't forget your teddy bear," her dad called.

_____ **1.** Which of these sentences is probably true?
  A. Jan wants to see how many socks she has.
  B. Jan doesn't like nightgowns.
  C. Jan is getting ready for a trip.

2. Your skin is made of a thick layer of tiny, living parts called cells. Your skin helps keep you alive. It holds in the moisture that your body must have. Sometimes skin from one part of the body can be put onto another part. This is called a skin graft. Skin grafts can help someone who has had a bad burn.

_____ **2.** Which of these sentences is probably true?
  A. Skin grafts don't work.
  B. Skin grows on only one part of the body.
  C. A skin graft can save a person's life.

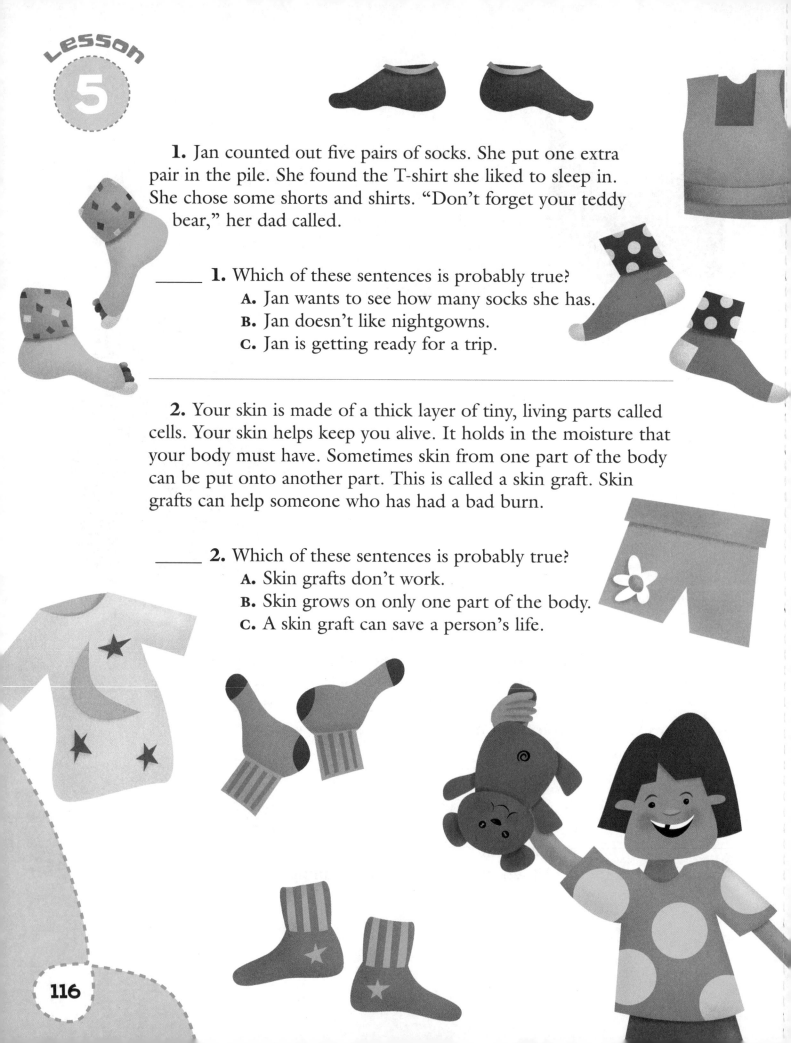

3. A cave is a hole under the ground. Most caves are formed in rock called limestone. Caves are made by water. Water eats away part of the rock. Over many years a small hole or crack in a rock becomes very big. Then it becomes a home for bears or bats. It also becomes a place people want to explore.

_____ **3.** Which of these sentences is probably true?
    A. Water collects in limestone cracks.
    B. Animals stay away from caves.
    C. Caves are open to the sun.

---

4. Could you buy an apple today with a seashell? No, but long ago you could. People used seashells as money. In Africa, you could buy a goat for 100 seashells. You can still find these shells on the beach. They are about the size of a bean. But don't try to buy an apple with them. They're not worth a penny.

_____ **4.** Which of these sentences is probably true?
    A. Long ago it was good to have many seashells.
    B. Today people shop with seashells.
    C. Wood is made from seashells.

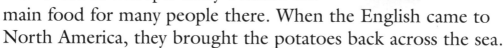

1. The Incas lived long ago in South America. They were the first people to grow white potatoes. They used them to make bread. People from Spain came to the Incas' home. When these people left, they took some white potatoes home with them to Europe. They became the main food for many people there. When the English came to North America, they brought the potatoes back across the sea.

_____ **1.** Which of these sentences is probably true?
- **A.** Potatoes can grow well in different places.
- **B.** The Spanish grew the first white potatoes.
- **B.** White potatoes taste like sweet potatoes.

2. Don and his dad walked into the bank. "Where does a bank get money?" Don asked. "The bank gets money from people like us," Dad said. "We put money into a savings account. Then the bank uses that money to cash checks or make loans to people. The bank's money comes from all the money that people put into bank accounts."

_____ **2.** Which of these sentences is probably true?
- **A.** The bank uses your money for many things.
- **B.** Banks print the money they lend.
- **C.** The government takes the bank's money.

3. Long ago, people made furniture, clothes, and tools at home. Each family worked together to make a certain thing. If you wanted to buy a table, you went to a family who made tables. Back then it took a long time to make things. Now tables, dresses, and other things are made quickly in factories. Then they are shipped to a store. You don't have to wait for what you want. You can just go in and buy it.

_____ **3.** Which of these sentences
   is probably true?
   A. Things are made faster at home than in a factory.
   B. People come to your home to make things.
   C. Today most things are not made at home.

---

4. A large truck pulled into the driveway. Four men got out of the truck. They pushed up the back door and rolled a large, black object off the truck. It had a set of white keys on one end. Two men pushed it, and two men pulled it. When it was in the house, they screwed on three legs. The men lifted it so that it was right side up. One man sat down to play a song.

_____ **4.** Which of these sentences is probably true?
   A. Playing the piano is easy for everyone.
   B. No one wants to move a piano.
   C. It takes at least four people to move a piano.

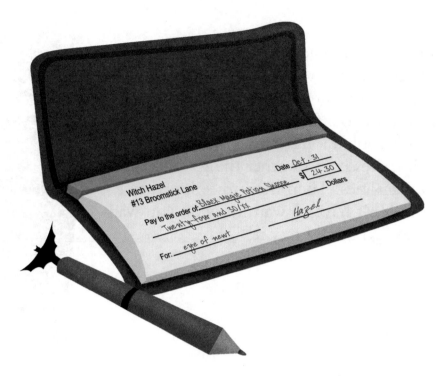

1. Every country makes money for people to use. People use coins that are made from metals. Coins might be silver or copper. Gold is too soft for a coin. People use paper money. Paper money might have pictures of kings, queens, or buildings on it. A check is a kind of money, too. A check means you have money in a bank to pay for what you buy.

_____ **1.** Which of these sentences is probably true?
     A. Money looks different in different countries.
     B. Silver coins are the only kind of money.
     C. A check is not as good as money.

---

2. Beth wanted to find out where her aunt lived. She looked at a map. She found the name of the town. Then she saw a star by the town. Her teacher told her that a star meant the town was the capital of the state. Beth looked at other states on the map. Each state had one town that was marked by a star.

_____ **2.** Which of these sentences is probably true?
     A. Each state has two capitals.
     B. Each state has one capital.
     C. Some states don't have capitals.

3. Sea turtles come out of the water to lay their eggs. The female turtle comes up on the beach when it is dark and no one is there. She digs a hole in the sand. She lays the eggs in the hole and covers them with sand. Then she goes back into the water. The baby turtles hatch in a few weeks. They hurry to get into the water.

_____ **3.** Which of these sentences is probably true?
    A. The mother sea turtle never sees her babies.
    B. Mother sea turtles live on land.
    C. Sea turtles stay to watch the eggs hatch.

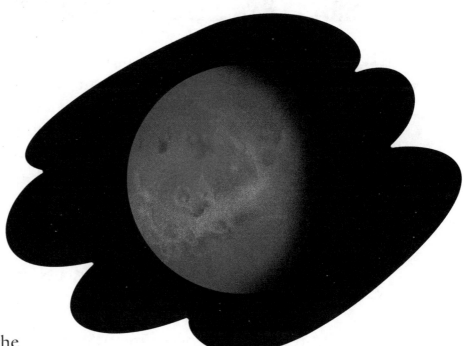

4. Venus is the second planet from the Sun. It is close to Earth. It is very bright. It looks like a star in our sky. Venus is almost as big as Earth. There are thick clouds in the sky. They hold the heat from the Sun. It is very hot. It is hot enough to melt a car. Venus has tall mountains. They are taller than any on Earth.

_____ **4.** Which of these sentences is probably true?
    A. Venus is bigger than Earth.
    B. You cannot see stars at night on Venus.
    C. It is easy to drive on Venus.

1. Jake and his dad took turns mowing the grass. They tried to cut it once each week. They used a mower with a sharp blade. After many weeks the grass began to look uneven after it was mowed. It was high in some places and low in other places. Jake looked at the blade. It was dull and needed to be sharpened.

_____ **1.** Which of these sentences is probably true?
　　A. Jake watched his dad cut the grass all year.
　　B. Water made the blade get rusty.
　　C. A sharp blade on a mower cuts grass evenly.

---

2. A dirt road changes over time. When it rains, water washes away some of the dirt. The road becomes very wet and muddy. Cars get stuck in the mud. They make big holes as they try to get out. When the road dries, it has big holes in it. When the weather is hot and dry, the dirt on the road cracks. Some of it blows away.

_____ **2.** Which of these sentences is probably true?
　　A. Weather can change a dirt road.
　　B. Water helps a dirt road stay smooth.
　　C. Muddy roads are fun to drive on.

3. Sam built a fence in his yard. He dug eight deep holes. He put a post in each hole. The posts would hold up the boards for the fence. Sam laid a board across the top of the posts. He used a special tool to see if the posts were all the same height. The tool was called a level. Sam did not start nailing on the boards until the level showed that each post was the same height. He wanted the fence to look just right.

_____ **3.** Which of these sentences is probably true?
   A. A fence should always be painted.
   B. A level helps you see if things are even.
   C. It is easy to make a fence.

4. In the fall the leaves fall off the trees onto the roof. Often they get stuck in the gutters. A gutter on a house catches rain as it runs off the roof. The gutter takes the rain away from the house. The rain runs down a pipe to the ground. If a gutter is filled with leaves, rain does not run away from the house. The gutters fill up, and the water spills over.

_____ **4.** Which of these sentences is probably true?
   A. Gutters hold water for plants.
   B. Things on a roof get washed into the gutter.
   C. Leaves help gutters drain water.

Writing Roundup

Read each story. Then read the question that follows it. Write your answers on the lines below each question.

1. Robert looked at the menu. Every dinner on it cost more than $15, and Robert had $10 for food. Robert put down the menu. He had to get out of there. He had to find a place to eat.

Why did Robert want to leave?

_____

_____

_____

2. Carla took her math book to the library. She made copies of some pages in it. She went home. Now she has the copies, but she doesn't have the book.

Where is Carla's book?

_____

_____

3. Koji got ready to play basketball. He pressed down on the foot pump. It was working. He pumped it up and down about 20 times. Was that enough pumping? One bounce would tell him the answer.

What was Koji doing?

_____

_____

Read the paragraph below. Then answer the questions.

The moving truck was two hours late. Aisha had hoped it would be on time. The moving man didn't have any helpers. Aisha thought he needed help. She did not see how he could do all the work. She thought about talking to the man, but she did not know what to say. The man didn't seem to be very friendly, but he hadn't done anything wrong. Aisha waited. She needed to see how the man loaded her things. She just hoped that nothing would be broken.

1. Why had the moving truck come there?

_____

_____

2. Why doesn't Aisha talk to the man?

_____

_____

3. What kind of person is Aisha?

_____

_____

4. Why does Aisha seem worried?

_____

_____

Check Yourself

Unit 1

Lesson 1
pp. 8–9

1. B	5. A
2. C	6. B
3. B	7. B
4. B	8. A

Lesson 2
pp. 10–11

1. C	5. B
2. A	6. A
3. A	7. C
4. B	8. B

Lesson 3
pp. 12–13

1. B	5. C
2. A	6. B
3. A	7. B
4. B	8. C

Lesson 4
pp. 14–15

1. C	5. C
2. B	6. A
3. B	7. C
4. A	8. B

Lesson 5
pp. 16–17

1. C	5. A
2. C	6. C
3. C	7. B
4. B	8. A

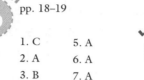

Lesson 6
pp. 18–19

1. C	5. A
2. A	6. A
3. B	7. A
4. B	8. C

Lesson 7
pp. 20–21

1. C	5. C
2. C	6. B
3. B	7. A
4. A	8. C

Lesson 8
pp. 22–23

1. A	5. A
2. B	6. A
3. C	7. A
4. C	8. C

Writing Roundup

p. 24

Possible answers include:

1. Humans have traveled there and brought back soil to study.

2. The soil is made of rock and glass.

3. Each glass bit is about as small as a period.

p. 25

Check that you have three facts in your story.

Unit 2

How to Find Sequence

p. 27:   2, 1

Lesson 1
pp. 28–29

1. 1, 2
2. A
3. C
4. B

Lesson 2
pp. 30–31

1. 1, 2
2. B
3. A
4. B

Lesson 3
pp. 32–33

1. 2, 1
2. A
3. C
4. B

Lesson 4
pp. 34–35

1. 2, 1
2. A
3. A
4. C

Lesson 5
pp. 36–37

1. 2, 1
2. B
3. A
4. C

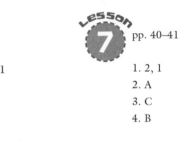

Lesson 6
pp. 38–39

1. 1, 2
2. C
3. A
4. B

Lesson 7
pp. 40–41

1. 2, 1
2. A
3. C
4. B

Lesson 8
pp. 42–43

1. 2, 1
2. C
3. A
4. B

Writing Roundup

p. 44

Possible answers include:

1. The frog eggs started to hatch after a week.

2. The tadpoles grew back legs in seven weeks.

3. The tadpoles grew front legs after they grew back legs.

p. 45

Check that your story is written in sequence.

Check that you have used time order words, such as first, next, and last.

Unit 3

How to Use Context

p. 47

In the story on page 46, the sentences "You're really good!" and "Go ahead and try to make the big time." should be circled.

Any words that mean *to help someone* may be written on the line. Words with this meaning include *to cheer up*, *to support*, *to back*, and *to help*.

 **pp. 48–49**

1. B	4. A
2. C	5. B
3. A	6. C

 **pp. 50–51**

1. B	4. A
2. A	5. C
3. B	6. B

 **pp. 52–53**

1. B	4. B
2. C	5. C
3. C	6. B

 **pp. 54–55**

1. C	4. A
2. B	5. B
3. C	6. B

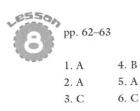 **pp. 56–57**

1. A	4. C
2. B	5. B
3. C	6. A

pp. 58–59

1. B	4. A
2. A	5. C
3. A	6. A

pp. 60–61

1. B	4. C
2. A	5. A
3. B	6. A

pp. 62–63

1. A	4. B
2. A	5. A
3. C	6. C

Writing Roundup

p. 64

1. afternoon	6. loud
2. leaves	7. careful
3. feed	8. true
4. glass	9. wide
5. joke	10. stood

p. 65
Possible answers include:

1. cold or snowy
2. coat or gloves
3. ball or stick
4. house or yard
5. back or tail
6. tree or bush

Unit 4

How to Choose a Main Idea

p. 67
Detail 1: bathtub, car
Detail 2: store
Detail 3: music while
    you sing a song
Detail 4: recording
Detail 5: take it home and surprise
Main Idea: Here's how you can
    become a singing star!

pp. 68–69

1. B
2. C
3. A
4. B

pp. 70–71

1. A
2. C
3. B
4. B

pp. 72–73

1. B
2. A
3. B
4. C

pp. 74–75

1. A
2. C
3. A
4. C

pp. 76–77

1. A
2. B
3. C
4. A

pp. 78–79

1. B
2. A
3. C
4. C

pp. 80–81

1. B
2. B
3. C
4. A

pp. 82–83

1. B
2. B
3. A
4. A

Writing Roundup

p. 84
Possible answers include:

1. Jessica McClure was lucky to be alive.

2. Not all presidents lived in the White House.

3. Gail Devers trained herself to be a runner.

p. 85

Check that you underlined your main idea.

Check that you used two details.

127

Unit 5

How to Draw a Conclusion

p. 87

Clue 2: A mother whale stays by her baby for about a year.

Clue 3: A mother whale feeds her baby milk.

Conclusion: Whales take care of their babies.

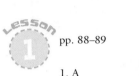 **pp. 88–89**

1. A
2. C
3. B
4. A

 **pp. 90–91**

1. C
2. B
3. A
4. B

pp. 92–93

1. B
2. B
3. A
4. B

pp. 94–95

1. A
2. C
3. A
4. B

pp. 96–97

1. C
2. B
3. C
4. A

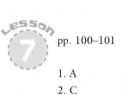 **pp. 98–99**

1. B
2. A
3. C
4. B

pp. 100–101

1. A
2. C
3. B
4. C

pp. 102–103

1. C
2. A
3. C
4. C

Writing Roundup

p. 104

Possible answers include:

1. Dorothy Kelly worked for an airline.

2. Some basketball shots are harder than others.

3. Mrs. Paz is the teacher.

p. 105

Possible answers include:

1. Tom opened the window. He said that he needed more fresh air.

2. Cody was inside his house. He watched the ball come into the house and land on the couch.

3. It was good that the window was open. If the window had been closed, the basketball might have broken it.

Unit 6

How to Make an Inference

p. 107

Fact 2: He hadn't washed his face.

Fact 3: His shirt was wrinkled.

Fact 4: One shoelace was not tied.

Inference: Sam doesn't care about how he looks.

pp. 108–109

1. C
2. A
3. A
4. B

pp. 110–111

1. B
2. C
3. B
4. A

pp. 112–113

1. C
2. B
3. B
4. C

pp. 114–115

1. A
2. B
3. B
4. A

pp. 116–117

1. C
2. C
3. A
4. A

 pp. 118–119

1. A
2. A
3. C
4. C

pp. 120–121

1. A
2. B
3. A
4. B

 pp. 122–123

1. C
2. A
3. B
4. B

Writing Roundup

p. 124

Possible answers include:

1. Robert didn't have enough money to eat there.

2. Carla's book is in the copy machine at the library.

3. Koji was filling a basketball with air.

p. 125

Possible answers include:

1. Aisha was moving.

2. Aisha doesn't want to talk to the man because he doesn't seem friendly. She wants to give the man a chance. She wants to see if the man knows what he is doing.

3. Aisha is careful and shy, and she worries about things.

4. Aisha is afraid that some of her things might get broken.

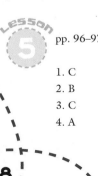